# POSITIVITY
## YOUR KEY TO
# SUCCESS

**Renny Roker**

Positivity: Your Key to Success by Renny Roker

Copyright © 2015 by Renny Roker

Cover by Ivan Thomas

188p. ill. cm.

ISBN 978-1-935795-38-4

LCCN 2015910705

_______________________________



Michael Ray King Publishing

PO Box 353431

Palm Coast, FL 32135-3431


Printed in the United States of America

# Table of Contents


Foreword

Preface  1

The Rhythm of Success  5

Teenage Businessman  7

Many Faces of Positivity  11

Through the Eyes of a Child  20

Americas Paradise Triathlon  27

Surviving the Storm  33

Children First, Money Second  50

Reinventing Yourself  53

It Pays to Have History  58

Nat "King" Cole's Last Hit Record  73

Fastrack  78

Busy, Busy, Busy, Chaotic (and Smiling)  82

Stax Records and ROHAM  85

Johnny Taylor Gold in California  87

Isaac Hayes' Academy Award  90

Donna Summer and Exlax  92

JAG BMX World Championship  95

The Mothership Tour  100

From Poop to President  103

Self Esteem  107

It Takes a Vision and a Great Team  110

# Table of Contents


Dreams Do Come True  115

People are Important  119

Big Time Chicago Concert  123

Bronx Zoo  126

Sisters and Brothers, Love and Hate  128

If You Can Dream It, You Can Do It  131

Lonely and Confused  133

Know Your Audience  136

Know What You Need  138

If You Believe  143

If at First You Don't Succeed  147

I Dream in Colors  153

Helping Each Other, Can You Help a Brother?  155

Getting a Royal Spanking  157

Choosing the Path of My Future  160

Create Loyalty to Keep Sponsors/Partners 164

Doing What is "Right"  167

Conflict Resolution  171

Positivity  174

About the Author  177

I dedicate this book to my Mother, Edna Lillian Roker, who lived for 29 years with Alzheimer's Disease, and the Lady of my life, Linda…

## Foreword

When I first met Renny Roker in 1987, he was attempting to do the near impossible. He had cobbled together a television studio in a dilapidated building on St. Croix in the U.S. Virgin Islands and convinced NBC Television Network to air a triathlon event he planned to host and film on the island the following year.

At the time, he didn't have the money or staff to pull it off. But the doubters and scoffers, and there were many, didn't know Renny Roker.

Rather than scale back the size or scope of the event, Renny raised the stakes. He offered the largest purse in triathlon history and began amassing a list of competitors that was a virtual who's who of the sport. In addition to the world's top triathletes, he would attract a 16-year-old cyclist named Lance Armstrong and a 12-year-old swimmer and later-to-be basketball legend Tim Duncan.

Putting on an event of this magnitude in such an unlikely venue involved nothing short of promotional alchemy.  But this is what makes Renny Roker the master promoter he is.

From convincing hoteliers to offer discounts and give comp rooms, to corralling Virgin Islands officials and businessmen, Renny used his easy charm and infectious optimism to rally a small army of volunteers and make the America's Paradise

Triathlon a staggering success. The televised event drew a huge national audience and earned its producers – Renny and company – a well-deserved Emmy nomination.

It was vintage Renny Roker! And when it was over, the near flawlessness of its execution made it easy for those watching from the sidelines to miss the magnitude of the accomplishment.

Over the years, I would see Renny make this magic again and again. It is his ability to reinvent himself and turn improbable ideas into soaring successes that make Renny Roker the ideal person to write a book on "positivity." It is, after all, his secret weapon.

Part autobiography, part entertainment industry history, the stories in this book weave effortlessly through the lives and times of some of the biggest names in show business. From his early days with Nat King Cole to his groundbreaking program for teen golfers from around the world, Renny lays out a blueprint for those hoping to emulate his success.

Positivity is the common thread woven into every chapter in this book. Here, in black and white, is the formula for turning even the most improbable dream into reality. This book is hardly an academic exercise in the theory of marketing and promotion; it is a firsthand account of a man who has created an enviable track record in the often-treacherous world of entertainment.

My advice is that you read this book on two levels. First, read it for the fascinating stories of Renny's interactions with some of the biggest names in business and the entertainment industry. Then read it as a how-to book, and follow the sage advice of a marketing and promotional guru who has lived a most improbable life by staying positive in even the most dire situations.

And always remember, the advice in this book is field-tested.

Positivity, and the boundless optimism it engenders, is the elixir that Renny used to transform himself from a struggling actor into a successful movie and record producer, record-breaking concert promoter, BMX (bicycle motocross) pioneer and television sports trailblazer. Renny freely dispenses the elixir of positivity in this book, with real-life examples of the power of practical optimism. It is hard to come away after reading "Positivity" without being inspired to go for your dreams, not matter how big.

~Melvin Claxton – Pulitzer Prize Winning Writer

# Preface

There is no question that your environment at home plays a role in your overall attitude, energy, and belief in yourself. At the same time, that person inside you plays an even greater role. When I was about four-years-old my family, mother, father, sister, brother and I lived in a two bedroom, walk-up flat on Ritter Place in the Bronx.

You could smell the urine on the walls when you walked in the main entrance. It was like living in a world with no windows or doors to get air. This home was my first real life lesson and I'll never forget it.

Giving up on yourself is the first step to disaster, while believing in yourself is the first step to success.  Staying positive has turned millions of people into success stories on many levels. There is no doubt in my mind that it certainly made a difference in my life.

The following story is the beginning of my realizing the power of "Positivity."

One Saturday morning I was in the tub taking a bath. My father walked in to tell me to get out of the tub. About the same time, a rat fell into the tub. My father yanked me out of the water and killed the rat with a plunger.

He called out to my mother to get herself and the kids ready to go to Long Island right away. When asked why, my father said "we're going to buy a house."

"With what money?" my mother responded. "You don't even have a job."

My father stiffened his back and calmly told my mom that after we found the house he would find a job. We loaded onto the train to the last stop in Queens, then the Q42 bus to the last stop. We ended up in St. Albans, Queens. The first house with a For-Sale sign was at 111-11 178th Street. Jackie Robinson, Roy Campanella, Count Basie, Lena Horne, Ink Spots, and many other celebrities lived just a few blocks away.

We walked in the front door and my sister, brother and I ran upstairs. Each of us claimed one of the three bedrooms out of four available. We discovered the living room, dining room, kitchen (all separate rooms), and if that didn't sell us, the basement did. It was awesome (lots of room for anything).

The deal maker for me was the backyard. It sported an apple tree, peach tree, pear tree, and grape vine. Lots of green grass and a fence spread beautifully around the entire yard. I was in heaven.

My dad gave the realtor his info plus twenty-five dollars as a deposit with a 120 day escrow. On Sunday my dad read the classifieds and plotted his employment seeking travels. My mom spoke of the twenty-five dollars my dad just gave away, but she also said to us "your dad is going to find a job and we're going to move into that house". That's positivity. My Mom and Dad had serious positivity.

On Monday at six o'clock in the morning, my father walked out of the door with two subway tokens and six cents in his pocket. I will never forget this day because it showed all of us the power of positive thinking and believing in yourself.

My father had the power of all that and much more in his heart and soul. You could see it on his face when he got home that evening with the biggest grin on his tired face. His stomach sounded off because it was completely empty.

My mother asked, "Reggie, you got a job?"

My Dad replied, "Kind of."

My Mother, (dejected) inquired, "Kind of?"

Dad explained, "In my first job I'm ironing pants for the Navy."

My Mother stated, "You never did that before."

"I looked through the window for two hours. When the man brought the handle down with the steam thing he would cause the steam to press the pants by stepping on the steam pedal. I watched and practiced outside till I had it down pat," my father said with a smile. "For my second job, I'm packing meat in the refrigerated trucks two buildings away. Right after that, I'm the night watchman around the corner."

As my mother digested all this, something told me we were going to move into that beautiful house. Two months later we moved in. I can still see the tears of joy in my mother's eyes, and a smile from ear to ear on my dad. I swore I could see a tear in his eyes.

Every Saturday morning about six o'clock, my dad would wake us up and give us chores to accomplish; from sweeping the sidewalk, pulling weeds out of the garden, or picking fruit. My mother canned or made juice, fruit pies or snacks from what we picked.

One day I asked, "Dad? You work five days a week, twenty-four hours a day. You get home at one in the morning on Saturday. At six o'clock in the morning, you have us cleaning, painting, weeding, sweeping, picking fruit…"

Dad cut off my spiel and looked me in the eyes to make sure I got his message. "I don't work twenty-four hours a day, five days a week to have the worst looking house in the neighborhood!"

It took me a few moments to get it; I mean really get the complete meaning of that statement. Even to this day, many years later, I still hear it, especially on those infrequent moments when physical or mind fatigue begins to creep in. It's like fireworks in the mind, body and soul saying "are you kidding me? Tired?" I keep on going forward and achieving.

Thanks Dad!

My hope is that each person who endeavors to read this will be blessed many times over by the enlightening, and enlivening messages throughout. Positivity is about believing in yourself and not being afraid to put your dreams into reality.

# The Rhythm of Success

Sometimes words need help, and the correct rhythm will add just enough meter to even an out of tune statement. Think positive, be positive, act positive.

You really have to concentrate in order to get something done. But when you are striving to be the best, sometimes you have to go the final mile all by yourself. Not because you have to do it alone, but because if you are going to truly be successful you must believe in yourself and you must do it for yourself.

Many will ask, "How do I do that?"

Real simple. It takes the tenacity, the energy, the desire, the education, and another component that is critical – rhythm. Yes. Rhythm. Why?

In order to dance to the music of success, you must have the rhythm to support the sweet melody that is necessary to find your groove and set the pace necessary to become a success.

I have seen young people who have what it takes to become successful. They often fail because they forget the necessary steps it takes to turn the corner that leads to the final dash to the finish line. It is important to follow the road map until it ends.

You must create and develop your road to the finish line. You must expose your interpretation of what is considered the rest of the road to success. Regardless of race, creed or color, that final road demands understanding and patience. Yes, patience with a "hurry up" gear needed to get you to the finish line.

Many will ask, "Is there a shortcut?" Well of course there is. There's a whole bunch of shortcuts, but ninety-nine percent of the time they lead nowhere.

To me, it is great to see youngsters making their way up the ladder of success. But it's not just the youngsters struggling up that same road. There are many twenty somethings, thirty somethings, forty somethings, fifty, sixty, and seventy somethings chasing that dream and praying hard for a chance. Any chance will do for many.

Any chance normally means an opportunity for the young, but it is very important to realize that there are many who are no longer young but still in need of an opportunity to a slice of the sweet, succulent, and satisfying feeling you get when there is success.

Regardless of your age or education level achieved, it is very important that you grasp the rhythm of the vocation you have chosen. Whether you pat your feet or dance all night, it is important you do not miss the rhythm of the vocation you have chosen. And keep the beat no matter what is going on.

Go ahead, tap your feet. Feel the rhythm. Sing the song. Make sure you don't miss a beat. I wish you success, I wish you good fortune. I hope you do not lose sight of where the dance will go, and how to get there.

It's amazing what a rhythm can do for an important request, for an important statement, for good health, for a great workout, and for peace of mind. The rhythm of positivity will serve your life well.

If you think positive, positive things happen and that is what positivity is all about.

## Teenage Businessman

Wow! What a lesson! Power used in a positive way can make a major difference in someone's life. I was living proof. This made me aware of the power of "Positivity" and still does today.

It really pays to understand exactly where you are as you secure positive outcomes, sales, or recognition. Keep moving forward as the reverse switch seems to always be ready to get in gear.

Positivity can take even the most negative situations and turn them into something fantastic. Positivity on its own, will always in the end, bring good things to your life. I took this advice and used it in every possible moment.

The decision was very simple. Work hard, study long, succeed with everything, especially good grades in school. Smile a lot in the proudest fashion possible.

In my pre-teen years, all the money I made went to my mom. Unknown to me she put this money in a savings account. For me. I deeply respected my parents and my brother and sister, but my mom was my favorite in the family. Both my mom and dad read books every day for knowledge and or entertainment.

It didn't take us kids long to realize the importance of education and the knowledge of whatever subject, or ambition was important at that time. I had a great habit of getting "A's" in every subject and "D's" with red circles around them in conduct. You see, I felt that I could teach the class as good as my teachers.

At one time, I was a teenage disc jockey, food deliverer, car wash guy, and paper boy (delivering papers on bike).I enjoyed working when I was young. The car wash was fun to me. I enjoyed meeting rich, poor, and middle income neighbors. Those that tipped big and those that could barely afford to get their car washed. Each had their own rhythm.

I realized that you are who you think you are, and it pays to be pleasant to everyone. That really helped me with my "Packages Assistance Program" also known as delivery boy service.

A group of us would bring our wagons, (some home-made, some store bought) to the local A&P Supermarket. From my wealth of experience at the car wash, I realized that tips were earned based on service, personality and good manners. It was amazing the difference in tips by just asking customers if they wanted you to bring the bags up the steps into their home.

I believe that's called "Quality Customer Service," which entails caring and understanding about your clients. Mine were mostly housewives and mothers of children just like me. When a mom said, "I wish my son would go do this for extra money," I immediately offered to help them get their youngster started.

Tips got bigger, and I became a personal delivery person. People actually waited till I returned from a delivery to take their packages home. "Positive Customer Service." I didn't realize then how important this would be later in life.

The job that literally brought me to my knees was my newspaper route. Folding papers, checking addresses, reviewing who paid and who didn't, and who complained they did not get their paper, etc. It became very clear early in my life that when I interacted with people, like at the car wash, I got the most tips.

I made twice as much as the other kids because of my "Customer Comes First" positive attitude and extra care. I carried the packages right into each home instead of the top steps or front porch. But newspaper delivery, never seeing your customer except to collect, was terrible.

My father had his first heart attack and the doctor recommended my mother get him to a more peaceful location to rest and recuperate. So we moved to my grandparents' home in the Virgin Islands. At eleven-years-old I was a year away from going to high school. I felt that I was already sixteen and deserved to be treated like an older guy by everyone, including my parents.

Oh my God! Outdoor toilets, no television, not even a theater with real movies! And forget 3D, which was the rage in New York. I buried myself into books. I visualized the book becoming real action characters. That's when I knew I wanted to become a producer, director and maybe even an actor. Yes! I could do that!

I could do anything I wanted to was my attitude. I hated and loved high school in the Virgin Islands. We had to wear uniforms, khaki pants, white shirts and burgundy ties for the guys, burgundy skirts and white blouses for the girls. This was not going to work.

Contrary to my belief, it did, in fact work! It worked for me and many other children on the island. Ninety-nine percent of all high school graduates in the Virgin Islands in those days went to college (no television, no theater, just books, clean air, and sunshine every day).

At thirteen, in my junior year, I won a teen radio contest that got me a one hour program on every Saturday. By the end of the first month I was the most popular youth market DJ in the Caribbean with (of course) the hottest show on the radio - The Renny "Dr. Jive" Roker Show (yep, I became Dr. Jive, my radio hero in New York).

All the kids called me Dr. Jive or Dr. Drive because I drove my own car to school each morning then to work, then home. On the weekends I pulled six-to-eight-hour shifts and hosted my own beach parties just below the studios. In my mind, I was the hottest thing on the radio. About this time, my brother was recording his third or fourth million-selling record in a group called The Heartbeats.

One day, leaving late for school, I was going close to 100 mph. It began raining just ahead of me on the highway. I hit the brakes and slid on the water slick road, destroyed the car, and eventually walked away with a very slight scar on my right calf.

Right after that, I became the poster boy for safe driving in the Caribbean. My advertisers loved it and increased their advertising on my program and my salary increased. Wow! Can you imagine?

Throughout all these early working days in my youth, I made a lot of positive decisions. When I followed through, good things happened. Do the right things, work hard and get rewarded, another lesson to be learned and practiced. Fortunately, as is true with positivity, sometimes when I made poor choices, good things happened as well because I corrected myself and did the right thing with positivity.

# Many Faces of Positivity

"Positivity" allowed me to meet and work with many incredible people, from the rich and famous to the sharp, intelligent, up-and-coming superstars in the music, motion picture, and television world. I say to all parents and young adults, "do everything you can to read about or meet the true hero's and/or stars in the industry of your choice.

Ask the questions, "How did you become successful? Is it still possible to do that now or is there a new way?" This is not a shortcut, it's reality in the real world. Knowledge for success from books and achievers is very important.

During my college days, I met Nat "King" Cole who later became my first boss in the music business. I promoted Donna Summer at Casablanca Records years after college. I was responsible for the first African-American produced sports series on network television, the JAG BMX World Championship Series 1979-85. I started the team and the sale of branded bikes. I got corporate sponsors following forty-eight trips to Atlanta to get Coca-Cola to be our title sponsor.

I earned a full scholarship to Inter American University in San German, Puerto Rico for Broadcasting/Speech. Mr. Dennis was head of the department and my instructor. My goal was to do it all when it came to music, film, television creation, production, promotion, and sales.

By that time, my Caribbean accent was so thick I was told to listen to top U.S. newscasters and record their newscast over and over and over. The goal was to make it possible for everyone to understand my Caribbean accent.

I was determined to make it. When I went back to New York after college, I would spend the day in my brother (Wally Roker) and Mr. Al Sears' office to learn the music business. I took small roles in off-Broadway plays on the weekends while working as a bus boy in a coffee shop in Queens, N.Y.

At times I would sit in the office of Clarence Avant, a New York businessman, who was from the Caribbean. He was extremely smart and powerful in the music industry. He was the minority representative for several United States Presidents, advising them on minority affairs. I was in his office once when he was speaking with John F. Kennedy. They talked as if they were old friends, and they were.

Mr. Avant was the first manager of color in the music business to make a million and then ten million dollar deals for a recording artist. My brother represented eight different major record companies for promotion and marketing. Opportunity was everywhere. My brother helped me get a job representing Nat "King" Cole's record company and Mr. Cole's records on Capital Records.

I spent most of my waking hours communicating with radio programmers and personalities in all fifty states day and night. I did everything I could to sell records.

Both Mr. Cole's partner in the record company and Capital Records decided that he should sing a Rock and Roll song. This idea was as wrong as Frank Sinatra singing rap.

I found a song called Ramblin' Rose, sent it to Mr. Cole and begged him to record it. A deal was created to put Ramblin' Rose on one side and a Rock and Roll song on the other. I was up against 300 Capital Record promotion personnel and staff (loved it)! This was the ultimate challenge. Score one for

Renny and Nat "King" Cole. Ramblin' Rose became Mr. Cole's last hit record.

Mr. Cole gave me a bonus I'll never forget. Then he fired me. He knew he would soon die, but before he did, Mr. Cole introduced me to incredible opportunities to enhance my future.

Mr. Cole introduced me to Otto Preminger and asked him to help me get work as an actor at Paramount studios. This connection resulted in more than 300 television programs, forty plus motion pictures, my own series on television - "Nobody's Perfect" – twenty-two episodes of Gomer Pyle, a recurring regular on Hill Street Blues for more than twenty episodes and I also had more than seventy-five commercials, and 100 voice-overs.

"No matter how secure and successful you think you are, it's important to make sure you have a Plan B, or other means of resources, or a definite place to insure a healthy income. Most of us tend to forget that nothing in life is definite, except death and taxes. Incredible success or failure is often just around the corner.

During a period where I was on an incredible roll. Everything seemed to be going my way, and then it went crazy, I had just finished filming a movie in Florida with John Schlessinger called "Honky Tonk Freeway." My next two movies were with lead or co-leading roles ready for pre-production, when the longest actors' strike in history began.

I had just purchased a home for me and my son in Lake Hollywood. It was awesome. As the weeks went by and small industry supportive businesses were folding, it was obvious we were in for the long haul. One by one each of my film contracts became null and void, (legal when there is a strike for more than six weeks). I still had a mortgage, my son, massive overhead and now no job.

One day I drove into town to meet an old friend, Cecil Holmes, who used to go to radio stations with me when I was with Nat King Cole. Cecil had become partial owner of a company called Casablanca Records.

Cecil gave me the grand tour of a house and garage converted into a really nice office in the middle of Hollywood. After the tour, we sat down and Cecil surprised me by declaring, "Renny I need you to help me."

I was thinking I need him to help me as I was running out of money. Christmas was close and I wasn't working. My son had a list longer than my arms of desired Christmas gifts. I asked, "Cecil, how could I help?"

"Come to work for me as an independent consultant and promotion director of my division. When you have a movie or television show or commercial to do you can do it."

It took me about five seconds to say, "Yes."

We talked about the job. He played me all the new songs coming out, including a wild new record by Parliament/Funkadelic, and another by Cameo. Cecil seemed to dodge the money discussion every time I tried to bring it up.

I heard all the stories about how they had struggled and were hoping for something big. Cecil sat me down in his office and said, "We'll pay you $400 per week. You can come and go as needed for your television or film jobs, as long as you are making calls while on the set of a television program, film or commercial."

I was stunned because I made more than that in a day! Now I was being offered this amount for a week's wages. My son's bike for Christmas was going to cost me close to a week's wages. This was just the beginning of what seemed like a bad deal. I still had my mortgage, taxes, food, and gas costs.

I knew Cecil, and his boss and major owner of the company Neal Bogart. I believed in these guys and knew they would do whatever it took to get this company going. By the time the strike ended we had a hit record with Cameo, and Parliament's record was about to be released.

Parliament's album was called "Chocolate City." I created a contest among every high school in every inner-city community. The rules were very simple. Students were to write, or draw "What Chocolate City means to me." The prize winner would get $500 and their school would get a free concert by Parliament/Funkadelic.

One day, Neil Bogart walked into my office and announced that here was more than a million pieces of mail coming into the office. "What the F--- is going on? Did we just partner with the post office?"

I replied, "No. We're selling records."

Neil was about to say something else when his sales manager ran into my small office and said "we just sold over 1.5 million Parliament albums! Distributors are going crazy, talking about some contest we got going and they want to support it."

Neil pointed at me and said, "Ask Roker, he's doing it." and walked out of the room.

Records were selling. Kiss. Donna Summer. Village People. Cameo. We were on fire. I got a nice raise!

Just as things can go bad, just as easy, as things can go great! One thing is for sure - if you begin with a positive, you are more likely to encounter more positives. Another lesson learned. Staying positive and increasing your awareness and increasing your positive base can only enhance your position in life. In less than a year, I went from flat broke to a lot of money in my bank accounts.

Another reason for staying positive was occurring. I was the recipient again. More importantly, so was my son. My son had won over 100 trophies by this time in BMX Racing and could not find a sponsor, so I started my own company.

Kelly (my son) named it JAG BMX. JAG BMX was a gamble. I knew enough about bikes to only get in trouble. I needed help so I went to the owner and president of Mongoose Bikes. I asked him to make a JAG BMX Bike. I told him I would promote both of us.

He agreed and we worked together. In 1979, we hosted the first JAG BMX World Championship in Indianapolis, Indiana. More than 4,000 youngsters from more than 65 countries showed up. We had signed sponsorship with Coca-Cola, Thom McAnn Shoes, 7-11, Bally Games, Mattell Toys, Veras Leathers (race clothes), Post Cereals and many others.

We barnstormed across the U.S. hitting at least thirty-five states, picking up local team members on every stop. We even made the cover of Ebony magazine on a stop in Chicago with the original team. We were very popular for a new company. Our guys and young ladies were winning in every city.

As youngsters joined our teams in each market, we made it very clear "they must have good grades to be on the team" or they would be asked to turn in their JAG BMX Jersey. I mention this because it was the reason we had the first youth sports series ever broadcast on ESPN "The Jag BMX World Championship Series." Positivity works again!

I had been calling, chasing and almost stalking a sports sales executive at ABC Wide World of Sports Division for a year. He avoided as many calls as possible. The ones he took were very short, and it was obvious that "No" would always be his response.

As a single parent in early 1979, I was sitting at home on a Saturday morning watching television when a call from the exec at ABC came in for me. "Hey Renny. How would you like to see Pele's last game tomorrow in D.C."

He offered me a limo to the airport, seats with producers up in the press and production box, a room in D.C., and a room in New York. I needed to bring a suit and tie to meet with Mr. Roone Arledge, the most respected name in sports television in the world. I, of course, accepted the offer.

He sent a limo for me to my house. When I arrived, he informed me that his wife was in love with me, his son wants to come to my house, and his wife has threatened to marry me.

I thought he was going crazy. I told him I didn't know his wife, nor his son, and said I was going back to California. He told me that he and his wife had bribed their son with all types of gifts if he got good grades, to no avail.

Then his wife came to him with tears of joy because Mr. Roker called and told his son to, "Get your grades up by next week or send back your jersey." His son begged his mother to get him a tutor to get his grades up.

When he heard my name, he muttered something about me and my bugging him about some television program for his JAG BMX company in December, and he didn't want to do it.

His wife told him to, "Help that man or I'll marry him!"

With that, he smiled and said tomorrow will be a great day for JAG BMX. Instead of one show on ABC Sports, we received twelve shows per year with three shows rebroadcast each month every weekend on ESPN, eighty-plus countries, plus all military bases and ships at sea broadcasting our own television series.

I became the first Africa-American to ever own and produce a sports series for ESPN and later ABC, NBC, CBS, Turner, and the Golf Channel. I was the first to own a full scale studio to produce, edit, stage, and broadcast facility. BET did a story about us and those facts prior to building their own facility.

All the time spent chasing television was also spent chasing sponsors. Coca-Cola was my number one choice. I took forty-eight trips to Atlanta from Los Angeles to convince them that our brand and our events were a great vehicle to sell Coca-Cola.

On my forty-eighth trip to Atlanta and Coca-Cola, one of the finest human beings I have ever met and known in life, Mr. Walter Dunn, embraced our JAG BMX Program, events and competition series on ESPN.

This relationship developed to my being dubbed the Youth Sports Representative of Coca-Cola. I traveled to seventy countries promoting Coca-Cola, including China, where we were the first youth sports group to ever go to China from the U.S. What a journey! Coca-Cola went on to sponsor many events of mine over a thirty year period.

The years working with Coca-Cola as an independent company were very exciting. Walter Dunn believed in us and we never let him down. During that period we produced the first three-on-three basketball series on network television (ABC). The Coup de Hoop Series competed in ninety-six U.S. cities and the big finale at Venice Beach in Los Angeles. Our Commissioner was Karim Abdul Jabbar. In the second year, the event was held in Las Vegas on CBS.

We also produced and owned the following:
The second most important triathlon in the world, the Americas Paradise Triathlon in the Virgin Islands (Lance Armstrong's first professional and televised event).

"Through the Eyes of a Child" was a television series (total of over 500 programs) on the CBS affiliate in the Virgin Islands and broadcast in more than twenty Caribbean countries. This series comprised the stories of the history of the Caribbean as told by youngsters of the Caribbean.

Teens on the Green television series appeared on the Golf Channel featuring events from around the world. Our "Teens on the Green" (TOG) youngsters challenged others in more than thirty-five countries.

We also had the first Triathlon Olympic Qualifier for North American teams in the U.S. Virgin Islands on Turner Broadcasting.

Some highlights I will always remember during this period in my life. Because of all these efforts, we made it possible for more than 3,000 youngsters worldwide to earn scholarships to college, based on grades first. I was part of motivational presentations worldwide to standing room only crowds of youth, adults, and seniors.

Being the first of my race to accomplish many positive feats, and most of all the positive results and opportunities we have made possible for the children and families of the world is very rewarding. Opportunities come when you open your arms, prepare in earnest, free your mind from negativity, and believe in yourself. Positivity in high gear!

**Through the Eyes of a Child**
**The first television series in the Virgin Islands and Tortola.**

In all my years in entertainment and youth activities
worldwide, it is very apparent that self-pride and perseverance
played a key role in success. It is especially important to
believe in what you are doing and why!

Renny

Every time I think about a television series called "Through the
Eyes of a Child" that I created while living in the most
beautiful place in the world, the Island of St John in the U.S.
Virgin Islands, it feels very special. The reason?

The show became a reality due to a Catholic Priest, local
mothers of young children, members of a respected family on
the Island, and teachers who had discussed in several different
ways the importance of creating something for youngsters to
do on their free time in this paradise.

My first thought was to create an after school program that
would keep them physically active, like swimming lessons, or
diving. During a conversation about St. John, I began to
understand the incredible history and romantic stories about
this Island of 2,500 residents.

More than forty percent of St. John was preserved to prevent
overcrowding. There was no television, no fast food
restaurants, and almost no crime of any type. I thought that St.
John was the perfect place to have children tell the story of its
existence, its charm, and the incredible beauty that was

everywhere. This included, but was not limited to, six of the most beautiful beaches in the world.

It felt like I was embarking on a dream project. It began by getting the word out all over the Island that we were looking for six kids that would make up our basic cast and add others based on the episodes.

We started with some very strong stories that included facts of which I was not aware. I learned that at the height of slavery in St. John and the Virgin Islands, the slaves on St. John revolted and did not allow the slave owners to return for a very long time.

The story of the slaves was the first story we tackled and even got Tortola, a neighbor island just a few hundred yards away from St. John, involved with a group of young thespians that rounded out our basic group of young actors.

I had a camera man that worked at the local cable network in St. Thomas to shoot the show and edit with me. The local station in St. Thomas, channel ten, a CBS affiliate, was our broadcast station. This type of programming was new to the Virgin Islands.

One of our programs in which my new cast in St. Thomas got excited about, was the plethora of pirates in the old days on St. Thomas. We dreamed up a story of a bunch of kids that thwarted the pirates from attacking St. Thomas. In this story, a group of youngsters board an old multi-mast pirate ship that happened to be sitting just off the shores of a beautiful beach.

As the story goes, the captain would place a gold coin on the deck the night before a raid on the Island. The cast was to go on this ship, discover, and then steal the coin. In the process they would lose the coin as they dove and jumped off the ship running away from the pirates who awakened too late to catch them.

One of the key thoughts in this program was to get the seventy-five percent of young Virgin Islanders (that could not swim) to see the ocean as a friend, not a foe and begin learning how to swim.

Our cast went off the ship into the ocean and swam underwater to distance themselves from the pirates' bullets, then swam to shore, successfully averting an attack. Since the pirates' gunfire awakened the town, they were chased out to sea.

After these two episodes aired, every school in Tortola and the Virgin Islands made viewing "Through the Eyes of a Child" mandatory. It became a part of each school's curriculum.

What was equally exciting was the number of parents and grandparents that followed the series. Even more were the calls and letters from all the other islands in the Caribbean that wanted an episode filmed on their island.

They say there is only one way to prove the true success of a television program. The most expensive commercial back then was $300. In the 6:00 pm newscast, "Through the Eyes of a Child" had grown to $3,500 per thirty-second commercial with a waiting list that included McDonalds, Tourism, Education, and many other notables companies.

I remember getting off the ferry from St. Thomas to St. John one day and about twenty-five adults, mostly women, were waiting for me to arrive. At first they looked hostile. I was prepared for a verbal attack.

It turned out that they wanted to know why "Through the Eyes of a Child" and the talented youth, that by now had become super stars on their respective islands, were not on stateside network television. They were aware of my television exposure on more than 300 network programs including "Hill Street Blues" on which I was a recurring regular. I traveled from the Virgin Islands to Los Angeles once a month to film an episode of "Hill Street Blues" as attorney Brown.

I told them we were in discussion with Phyllis Tucker Vinson, first African American woman to head up an entire department of a major network (NBC). Her time slot was the only NBC time slot at the time that was number one in viewership. Phyllis and I had been discussing creating a "Through the Eyes of a Child" series for NBC.

The idea was to set an after school time slot that would broadcast once a week, with every other week featuring a story from the Caribbean and our local crew of talent.

Phyllis was as excited about her new position as I was in becoming an owner/producer of a television series that had substance. This was also a great opportunity for young people to perform, learn, and enjoy the history of their ethnic group in America.

I was going to Los Angeles to film a "Hill Street Blues" episode in two weeks, so we agreed that would be a great time to meet and conclude our agreement. When I arrived in Los Angeles, Phyllis was on a plane to South Africa with her husband.

She had quit because the network reneged on certain portions of her new position. I couldn't believe what had happened. I was directed to her replacement, a young brash man that was so full of himself I felt nauseated. He was there by default and lasted only thirty days, but he let me know he was not going to do anything Phyllis had approved.

I filmed my "Hill Street Blues" episode, went horse-back riding with my son, and returned to St. Croix where we taped the most incredible episode ever in the history of the series.

At this point, and I try to convey this especially to young people, I was ready to attack this episode with every fiber in my mind and body. On St. Croix there were identical twins that were on the Olympic swim team for the Virgin Islands along with Tim Duncan, the now famous basketball star.

We created a story with the help of a friend of mine who wrote the script about a young man from the 1970's and a young man from the 1880's which depicted their lifestyles. One was a spoiled brat on the swim team and the other a caring young man who swam to freedom.

In this story, the two boys meet on the beach as the young man from 1880's is being washed up on shore. Immediately they begin a journey that educates each other in a manner that both humbles and provides respect for each other.

The 1880's boy preferred to ride a horse into town rather than ride in a car, to using his conch shell to reach someone rather than a pay phone. The show was engaging. But the three moments that really stand out is when the two boys are sitting in front of a school watching all the kids in uniform exiting. The 1880's youngster was amazed at the number of kids of color attending school.

The 1980's youngster states how "he hates school" and the 1880's kid says, "I'm not allowed to go to school." As the conversation continues, the 1880's youngster tells the other how he was brutally beaten by his dad for telling him he wanted to learn how to read and one day become governor of the Virgin Islands.

His dad told him, "We can never be governor because we are black, and we must never learn to read or our masters will beat us" In that moment, the 1980's youngster finally understands and they go to meet the real Governor of the Virgin Islands, a black man.

The response was so overwhelming to that episode; we had to repeat it several times. First time I viewed the episode (after editing), I cried quietly, tears running down my face. I may have lost NBC but I gained a new respect for those of my race that endured pure hell every day of their lives.

I realized as the grade point averages took a humongous rise after the telecast, what we had accomplished. We didn't get NBC but we did get the pride of thousands of youngsters at home.

As I look back on that series, I realize the incredible impact we had and the potential for a film that could be incredible, especially in this day and age where the Housewives of Any City, Bachelors, etc. are considered worth viewing.

Men vying for some supposedly lucky woman, teenage mothers becoming a must-watch in many homes, and the History Channel featuring wars between junk dealers as their hit programs scream we need something of substance.

It is very easy to understand why this series was so popular, but it's more important to understand why a reasonable facsimile is needed today before our youngsters think early pregnancy, tattoos, bad language, cheating parents, lewd conduct, is what is needed to be successful.

Placing education, good recreation, and some mind-challenging academic problems to solve as a good way to make it in this world in front of our youth is far more beneficial.

In my heart, I know there is a plethora of great young people of every color and ethnic background that we can turn into heroes of today. By being aware of these youngsters, and utilizing the many creative tools available from music, to art, dance, to theater, we can make wholesome success through intelligence and positive morals.

Of course, lots of fun is a great way to instill this in the minds, hearts, and creative juices of our young and not so young. If we understand and respect ourselves and place a value on who we are, rest assured that value can only be raised, because no one else will raise your value for you.

When you instill positivity in yourself, you may inspire the same in others. The fact we were able to reach so many young people and impact their lives shows the power positivity brings to this life. I encourage you to keep this thought close to your heart.

## Americas Paradise Triathlon

Just because you face a lot of challenges and few people believe you can deliver, if you believe it can happen, follow through and don't give up. Positivity can carry you through anything.

One of the former race directors of the Boston Marathon was the race director for my "Americas Paradise Triathlon" in the Virgin Islands.

He said to me after our event was over, "Renny, you never questioned what we did for your event. You asked about unique and extraordinary things you wanted, to give it a greater story for viewers on television and spectators on the course. When I looked at the television broadcast, I finally saw what you saw and what many thought could not work. Doubters were taking credit for the idea. From now on I'm calling you Mr. Roker because you earned my respect!"

I will never forget the day we opened our studios in St. Croix in the Virgin Islands, "Paradise Productions." We had a soundstage for full production of the television series, commercials, and other produced programs.

We had four edit bays for post-production of quality programming, several cameras and sound packages, and even setups for helicopters and motorcycles and pickup trucks etc. We were ready to produce a triathlon for television with great visuals, colorful settings and unusual and beautiful bumpers showing off our location. Why, we even built steel band equipment and showed them playing for the crowd.

Let me make this perfectly clear. We had over five million dollars in the studio in 1987. We had a network contract, the best athletes from around the world, and, at the time, a little known teenager named Lance Armstrong.

We had every male and female winner from the Ironman for the past fifteen years, and just about all that finished in the top five. We had the largest purse ever paid in a triathlon up to that time. Every road in the event was freshly paved within thirty days before the event.

Dion Warwick was singing the national anthem and two NFL quarterbacks who played in Super Bowls, Warren Moon and Jim Kelly, were present. They even played golf with many of the triathletes.

Pulitzer Prize winning writer Melvin Claxton, who represented the Gannet owned Daily News newspaper in the Virgin Islands, created a series of pre-event stories that got radio and television locally to support a massive pre-event media blitz.

Thirty days out from the event, twenty-five to thirty athletes from Germany arrived to begin training. They included Wolfgang Detrick, who was first out of the water in the three-and-a-half-mile swim. When the German athletes arrived the "buzz" was on and we had a serious problem. All the hotel rooms were booked and we still had over 200 athletes without booked rooms.

But let me go back a minute because a friend that was at ABC when we signed to bring BMX to television was now at NBC. We went back and forth on whether or not they would broadcast our event. I asked him a very simple question "What if we began this event on one island and finished on another?

The response, "You got a deal! Meet me in San Diego in five days we'll discuss and finalize." We signed an agreement on the back of a napkin in a coffee shop in San Diego.

I was worried for the first time about my event with 200 athletes, plus some boyfriends/girlfriends with no rooms. Just as I had internally decided this was not going to be ok, one of our female volunteers and a friend walked into my office excited. She was invited out by a triathlete from South America and wanted my advice.

I told her my problem and she replied that she would adopt four of them, best looking between twenty-five and thirty, half jokingly. I jumped out from my desk, ran around it, and kissed and hugged her, yelling down the hall, "We will adopt an athlete!"

As my staff filled my office, we got friends and families on the phone looking for good homes for 200 athletes. This process took less than five days with us broadcasting on the radio along with Melvin's newspaper stories. Our "Adopt an Athlete" program was a huge success.

The on-camera staff arrived a few weeks prior to the event. When they arrived, we let them look at some of the footage already produced in our studio for the program. They were elated, but we had a visitor from the network that was ready to find problems.

Ok, let me go back again. When I signed my contract with NBC, they asked that I work with a staff location person since this was my first program with the network. This might sound strange, but the lady that was appointed for our project was the toughest taskmaster at the network.

She was convinced that a bunch of guys like us (we won't go racial) could not deliver a network show. She was amazed at the equipment we said we had and the first thing she wanted to do on arrival was inventory it.

With that completed she wanted to see the pre-event "bumpers" we pre-taped for the show, and she definitely wanted to meet our twenty-two-year-old editor which she felt could never edit a network one hour special.

After 'day one' of appeasing her every demand, we took her out on the course. She told us there was no way we could cover this course. We told her we had fifteen cameras and crew with three in the water and two under water that converted to land cameras for the run (last stage of event).

We had two helicopters especially for the narrow beach road athletes would attack on bikes leading up to our famous "Beast," an incredible hill. On the day of the event she wanted to be on the beach for the start, and on a boat or helicopter for swim. We accommodated her and she did all three.

She wanted to be with lead bike, so we put her with the second bike and she complained, but we knew the second bike would catch the first bike. We were able to show the distance between the two and the pass from second to first was dramatic and incredible. We lost her after the event because she was understandably tired.

For the next three weeks after the event she looked over our shoulders as the show was compiled and put together. Although we were not finished, she came downstairs to my office. She announced her departure back to New York.

She kind of apologized for not believing we could do this. I thanked her for coming and told her "You are the best person the network could have sent on our first show."

She asked me why I said that and I told her, "If we had tied our shoes wrong it would be in her report. Instead, you'd think we might win an award or two. If you feel that way as well, we'll probably win three or four awards." For the first time, she smiled and walked out the door. We won six awards for our program.

There were many lessons to learn from this project:

1. Do not panic, at any time

2. Believe in yourself and your staff

3. After you have checked everything, check again

4. Spend the extra time and/or money to be sure all equipment is in great shape

5. Have a plan "B" just in case

6. After people have their assignments, believe in them. Let them work with full authority to do the job.

7. Applaud people during the heat of event, especially when they are being pressed the most to perform.

8. If you know someone is in need of help, send help and additional hands if they need them. Allow them to delegate what needs to be done.

9. When it's all over and you are receiving accolades, be sure to share them. Let the entire world know how you feel about those people behind the scenes that you appreciate them.

There was a ten-year-old volunteer that ran to the side of the road to help a man on the run. He even gave him extra cold water sponges, and a piece of fruit. We included him in the broadcast doing this great deed. I believe he's still showing that to his friends.

Lastly, smile at the naysayers and pay attention to what you must do to do a great job. When it's over, the final product will speak for itself - and you. Our event was so successful that the Iron Man wanted us to work with them. It is now more than thirty years since we started this event, and the only interruption was Hurricane Hugo which took four years to recover from.

We changed our position so we could produce a ninety-six city, three-on-three basketball series (Coup De Hoop) for ABC, and the first U.S. Official Olympic Qualifier for triathletes on the neighboring island of St. Thomas.

Producing both events was really difficult, but it worked. Our pre-event program featured choirs of forty-five churches walking from every street leading to the waterfront as the sun set, with lit candles and singing as they walked. The Hallelujah Chorus filled the waterfront in song as they met the world famous Rev. Bobby Jones Choir on the waterfront.

Fireworks accompanied the end of the famous song and the crowds went wild. You should have been there. Hallelujah! By the way, the winner of the first Americas Paradise Triathlon won the Olympic Qualifier.

Is there a message in all of this? A contract written on a napkin in a small coffee shop in San Diego, California between a brash kid raised in New York and the Virgin Islands with a network executive (hoping he made the right decision), became a marriage of creative and innovative production that pleased millions of viewers.

For me the message is very simple. There is no such thing as a bad idea if you have given enough thought, reasoning, and preparation for success and checked yourself and the project at least twice before beginning executing. Once you have decided you're going with it, don't stop, don't quit. Stay positive. You know what it could be. Make it happen!

## Surviving the Storm

Devastating circumstances often become a breeding ground for negativity and failure. The ability to remain positive and forward-thinking will serve you far better, and often yield results you could never imagine.

Picture this. You have just signed a contract to produce the finals of a three-on-three basketball playground series in Venice Beach, California. You are the first to put Playground Basketball on network television.

"Coup de Hoop" was indeed the first playground series on network television. You have agreed to host qualifiers in ninety-six cities in the U.S. on the same day with a guarantee of New York, Chicago, Detroit, Newark, Atlanta, Miami, San Francisco, etc.

The real story is, how did this take place? You were the first to produce and televise an Olympic Qualifier for Triathlons in the U.S. You couldn't have picked a more difficult and dangerous course. Not only was it a success, the show ranked in the top ten of any event activity ever produced in the Virgin Islands.

You also moved a Harlem Globetrotters event in less than thirty days from the Virgin Islands to the Bahamas without a phone or a bank account (all banks were closed due to Hurricane Hugo).

The airport was partially closed, there was no running water or electricity, your studio was destroyed, a loss of over one million dollars in cash, plus five million dollars in equipment and an "out of business" insurance company.

Sometimes you are thrown a curve ball, fast ball, or sinker ball after hitting home runs. In life we all face adversity. It's not what it does to you, it's what you do to it.

You stand up to adversity, stare it in the face for recognition, then go make something positive happen, then something else. And something else. And yet something else. You will soon find out the recession of your life has become the best time of your life.

I was in a presentation meeting with the head of Sports Programming for ABC's Wide World of Sports, Roone Arledge. He was one of the true gentlemen in the industry, and a believer in Renny Roker. His assistant was in the meeting with us.

I presented everything I had. I was turned down on every project I had. He was not difficult to communicate with nor did he make me uncomfortable. He ended the meeting with, "You are welcome to come to me with anything you are excited about."

As I was walking out the door, his assistant said, "too bad you don't have something on basketball." That's when all the lights went on.

There are times in life that being in total control of all your faculties, especially clear thinking and remembering, are very important. This was one of those times.

The night before that meeting, my two sons Kelly and Royce and I were in a bitter battle. We were arguing over which city had the greatest playground basketball players in the world. The dispute was left with no one winning our fun argument.

"I do have something in basketball! (I knew I had to speak fast yet very clear, cause this was my out-of-the-door presentation). I have "Coup de Hoop" the ultimate playground championship in America in ninety-six cities at the same time, leading to regional championships and ending with the finals in Venice Beach. We can have the event on the outdoor basketball courts on the beach next to the body builders. The winning team gets $50,000."

Roone looked me dead in the eyes and said "Make it $100,000 and you got a deal!"

I practically fell over. I'd just spent over an hour trying to sell every sports discipline he enjoyed. The date was set for the following year.

We spoke about the Triathlon, which was on NBC, and then I got real brave with his love of basketball. "How do you feel about me producing the Harlem Globetrotters this year in the Virgin Islands (oh, I was really warming up now). We'll build a portable court on the beach, and the team can go for a swim during half time. I will have two palm trees holding the backboard, and at half-time or early third period I'll have five Mocko Jumbies challenge the Globetrotters.

He looked at me like I was crazy. "Ok, so what is a Mocko Jumby?"

"You ever see those guys that walk around on stilts in Caribbean Parades? Some of them are as tall as twenty feet on those stilts!"

He smiled and said, "I love it, and instead of throwing a pail full of paper or cloth they can throw sea water."

"Exactly," I replied. "We can have a special bathing suit section for just that part of the program. The fans will love it."

He stood up at his desk and threw his fist in the air. "Oh yes, this is great! We can bring our ratings back up with this program. Renny, you would have walked out of here with your two best ideas in your pocket. Were you saving those for the other networks?"

"Oh no!" I replied. "I'll get you a write-up so we can get contracts going right away, right?"

"I want them on my desk by tomorrow, right?"

"Absolutely!" I said, and almost skipped out the door.

Here I was, the only African American producing network sports events that he owned, for a major network, and now NBC and ABC and ESPN was carrying my programs.

"Oh my God I'm going to scream!"

I'm the guy who had a rat fall in my tub in the ghetto just thirty minutes from where I stood in the corporate office of the number one sports network. Talking about black and proud, I was the poster guy of the week, but I needed to get to work. How the hell did I come up with ninety-six cities in the same day? I must be crazy!

I called a good friend of mine in Chicago, Abe Thompson to coordinate the Midwest, then another friend for the thirteen western states. Hey this wasn't that bad! It was like having a great song come together and everyone applauding.

Ok, great, but first things first. I still had a Triathlon to get done in St. Croix, needed to book the Harlem Globetrotters for early December on the beach in St. Croix after hurricane season, but we haven't had a hurricane in more than sixty years, I heard recently.

Then I will begin early summer next year with "Coup De Hoop." Oh my God! You go Roker! I was smiling from ear to ear. With my studio, I could save lots of money doing all my post production there. My partners are going to go crazy with joy.

The Triathlon was a huge success, and the government was ecstatic about the results, especially since we had a repeat of millions of dollars in real estate sales, every hotel sold out, and those families housing athletes had a great time showing athletes the Islands.

Now that the triathlon was behind me, the Globetrotters were next in line. I sold a million dollar sponsorship to Thom McAnn Shoes with the understanding that any family with two adults and children would not only get in for free, but they would all be entitled to fifty percent off shoes for each person attending. They would get the certificates when they entered the arena.

We had begun rehearsing the Mocko Jumbies to challenge the Globetrotters. This was going to be fantastic! I just knew I had finally arrived as a true sports producer for network television.

Oh, did I tell you, I had also sold a million dollar sponsorship to Coca-Cola for Coup de Hoop and a $500,000 sponsorship to Reebok. They were promoting a shoe in our honor called "The Blacktop Playground Shoe."

As teams were getting ready to win the $100,000 prize, we also added a bonus of $5,000 each for any players in the finals wearing the Reebok Shoes. "It don't get any better than this," I thought.

It was heating up now because the Globetrotters and Coca-Cola came on board, as did the St. Croix Tourism Department. Other sponsors were getting in this wild event because it was going to be free for families and on network television. How hot is that?

The Globetrotters, according to their management, were excited that this could be the breakthrough event for them to regain their audience supremacy they once enjoyed years ago.

I was living the dream in my own home town (I adopted St. Croix because as a teenager I was very popular there in sports, ladies, cars, and my own radio show. Now I had returned, built the first full production studio ever in the Virgin Islands, and was back on the radio. I had a successful network event with the Globetrotters and a massive three-on-three "Coop de Hoop Championship" with plenty of sponsors.

Then I start right back with the Triathlon, and in between I was a recurring regular on the Hill Street Blues television series as Attorney Brown.

I had a beautiful house in a secluded wooded area with a 13 mile view of the coastline. It was a great place to dive the incredible "Wall" of St. Croix, an underwater magic show of plants and rock structure plus unique sea life just minutes down the hill from my house. Who could ask for more?

I had flown to Los Angeles to film a segment of Hill Street Blues and was at my house in Thousand Oaks, California when I saw a news flash about a hurricane named Hugo headed toward the Caribbean. The path looked like it would go through St. Croix and Puerto Rico, but it was still too early to predict.

I called my son, Kelly, who had moved down to St. Croix. He was living with me at the house on the hill. My son was strong as an ox, gentle as a lamb, loved by everyone, and had a wonderful girlfriend, as well as a great job. He was called "Ice Man" when he was eight-years-old because he was so cool. Not gangster or hoodlum cool, he just didn't panic about anything.

I should have known better than to ask him if everything was ok with the storm coming. "Everything is fine dad. Enjoy

California and take your time coming back." That was my warning that everything wasn't ok and that I better get back.

On that same night, the weather report was that the storm, which by this time had totally destroyed four other islands seemed to be going in a direction that would miss the Virgin Islands and Puerto Rico, but drop quite a bit of rain.

I was celebrating at that point because the rain would turn what was already a lush and beautiful island into a spectacular body of beautiful plants and flowers and trees with all the fruit trees laden with plump mangos, soursop, guava, and other Caribbean delectables. Hell, maybe I'll serve free healthy living fruit to the fans at the Globetrotters event!

My son had me calmed down. The storm was not coming. I was so excited about bringing the Globetrotters on network television to the island I knew as home, St. Croix.

Although I was feeling better, I kept one part of me looking at the weather report and the other selling more sponsors, and getting more reasons to give away more tickets. I decided that every family on the island (meaning adults and kids) would get to see the Harlem Globetrotters for free, even if I had to add another day.

I would add it for all those deserving youngsters. "Think positive Roker," I told myself. This has got to work and the storm will avoid St. Croix like it has for the past sixty-five years. Imagine going sixty-five years without a damaging storm in the "Hurricane Alley" of the world.

Two days before the storm was to hit the islands, my son called and told me that he was locking up the house and going into town to stay with his girlfriend's family because the storm was going to hit. The storm would definitely hit the homes on our side of the mountain.

I called every airline in the world trying to get home but nothing was flying into that area. Instead of being there, I was going to watch it on television (not good). I received one more call from my son. He had made it into town and he would see me when I got there after the storm because the airports were all closed.

One, two, three, four days after the storm, I still could not get through to anyone including the radio and television stations. Neither the Governor's office nor any of my friends had any power, no utilities, and no telephone.

I finally got a flight five days later. On the landing, one thing was very obvious - there were no leaves on any trees. The sight was haunting - my beautiful island with leaves atop all trees like a bushy haired forest, this time they were all bald.

What else lie ahead? A friend gave me a ride into town and refused to drive up to my house, giving all kinds of excuses why he wouldn't. I was told by a taxi driver that every house on my mountain was gone, blown away. On the ride into Christiansted, there were homes with no roofs or windows and doors.

Ok Mr. Producer, Mr. Promoter. Spin this one! I didn't see one tree with leaves. So much for the trees holding the backboards for the Harlem Globetrotters idea. Was my son ok?

I found him and thanked his girlfriend's parents for allowing him to stay there. We jumped into the truck and headed to our house in the mountains. Trees were down everywhere.

I remembered I had all my gold records hanging on the walls in the house. I mentioned it to Kelly and his response was if the house is there the gold records are there. The more we climbed the worse it looked. Not one of the thirty-four houses on our mountain was there.

We were only halfway to our house. Household items from refrigerators to windows to bath tubs were strewn everywhere. We had to move trees and household items out of our path in order to drive. We couldn't see our house, even if it was there, so we drove quietly as Kelly pointed out all the places that used to have a home.

When we arrived at our u-turn driveway and started down the hill, there it was, the only house left standing on the hill! We couldn't drive down the hill, so we walked over and around the fallen trees.

My mind was racing. How do we promote the Globetrotters event with all of the trees on the beach without leaves and branches? Most appeared that if you leaned against them, they would drop. The real question now was how much damage control could we do here at the house?

We had no electricity, no running water, no food, but everything was in place. The front doors were each nailed to the wall wide open. All the gold records and awards were still on the wall. Everything was in place like it was when I left.

I asked my son why he nailed the front door to the wall and left the house open. Even all the louvered windows were wide open.

"Dad, the front side of our house is a screened in porch. There are no windows. All other sides are louvered windows. If a 100 mile-an-hour wind or stronger comes through the front with nowhere to go, the roof goes first, then the walls, then everything in the house."

"Brilliant, brilliant, brilliant," was my reply. "Mr. Cool" Kelly Roker had nailed it again.

The time came to call ABC and cancel the program, cancel the Globetrotters, and cancel the event, but there were no phones anywhere on island that worked. Two days later word went out there were phones downtown for long distance calls to friends and relatives.

I figured I could make my friend at ABC a relative based on the circumstances. When we got to town there were about 400 people waiting in line to make a three minute call on ten phones. I waited for what seemed like a day to get on the call.

By the time I got through to his office I was already a minute into my three minute call. John did not want to hear what I was saying. He said, "You got me into this you get me out of it. I'm sending down a few people in our company jet to take a look and see. Call me back in ten minutes and give me details."

In thirty seconds I explained the phone system and about how long it would take, "Ok I'll wait," he said.

When I finally got to the phone again, he had called the Harlem Globetrotters office. They were also following the storm and looking for alternatives. He told me to "call this number in Los Angeles and they will give you a number in the Bahamas to call, to make a deal and save your young life in television sports production."

I had one minute left. I called the number and quickly explained my phone situation, and asked that they have all details by the numbers so they could notify the Bahamas if we were going to go there etc.

Vincent Vanterpool Wallace was co-president of the hotel that wanted our event. He was willing to send a jet to pick me up and bring me to the Bahamas home of my father. Nassau had totally avoided the storm, and the hotel was beautiful and bigger than any hotel in St. Croix. The beach was ok, but we could get the job done. This was going to be great.

Once there, we went out behind the hotel to view the beach for the basketball set-up for the Globetrotters. We were able to identify a location that one side of the court would be over water. The great thing was that at half time we would have the Globetrotters jump into the ocean.

After a review of the grounds, we went back to Vincent's office to discuss details. Vincent let me know they would pay for all production, meals, hotel, etc. and they would give me $4,000 for signing over the contract to them.

I almost fell on my face. I had just returned a million dollar check to Thom McAnn for this event and now I was being offered $4,000 plus room and board and transportation. Vincent promised me he would take care of me in another promotion one day. I never thought I would see that day.

Surprisingly enough, he paid me $400,000 for a Luther Vandross concert weekend that brought more than 7,000 people from Florida and other locations to the Bahamas.

It was game day for the Globetrotters, and the parade of cars, bikes, busses and vans, not to mention the folks in the hotel were incredible. One of the Globetrotters was from the Bahamas and that made it even better.

At last it was happening and I had saved myself with ABC Sports. I might add that ABC gave the Virgin Islands a check for $75,000 to help families in need following this hurricane disaster.

At half time I wanted to see if the Globetrotters would really go into the ocean. Not only did they go into the ocean, they took about ten people from the crowd with them. It was a great day in the Bahamas. But the best was yet to come.

Not only did the Harlem Globetrotters program become a huge hit and the most watched Harlem Globetrotters telecast in history with six repeat broadcasts, it became the most played Globetrotters television program in their history with ABC Sports.

I was happy for the Bahamas and I was also happy that I was able to bring a donation from ABC to St. Croix. But I still had a million dollar plus loss due to the hurricane, no running water at home, no phone, no electricity, and no neighbors.

My son and I found an old plant-watering pail with the holes at the end of the bucket, and found a way to pour it over each other for a nice cold shower. We had ordered five generators that never arrived.

I had a few problems at first with my sponsors because our communications were terrible due to the fact our generators never reached the Virgin Islands. They only got as far as Puerto Rico. By the time a generator came I had to leave and begin the promotion on "Coup De Hoop"

We had been endorsed by Karim Abdul Jabbar. He became our "Commissioner" for the entire series, and even showed up at the finals which were standing room only at the Venice Beach Basketball Courts.

The event was really wild because we had hard rubber tiles that spelled out "Coca-Cola Coup de Hoop Basketball Championships" in bold red and white. Thousands rimmed the court as teams played for the $100,000 purse and the opportunity for potential tryout at one or more professional teams.

It literally went down to the last basket where a team from Florida won it all. (So much for large inner city kids from New York, Chicago etc. winning this event. Both me and my boys were wrong).

So the first year was in the bag and it was time for planning the next year of hoops. I called my buddy at ABC and he was excited. It went great and he told me to meet with him in about forty days as he was going to Europe with his daughter.

It was a shock and sad moment when I found out that the plane was shot down and they both left us forever. He was a gentleman and a person that cared about others. He liked to work with people who cared enough about themselves to do their best for their potential audience - always!

Fortunately, in our second year, CBS broadcasted Coup de Hoop and then NBC bought "Hoop It Up" for four million dollars. I immediately called CBS when I heard the news and asked if CBS would like to own us. Not only did they did not want to own us, they were cancelling the show. There was a lesson for me.

But to show you how different things are from back in those days here is a true story. When we went to Vegas with Coup de Hoop, our event was to be held in the parking lot of the Excalibur, a huge hotel with over 4,000 rooms.

My event was on their marquee in front of the hotel with a giant Pepsi-Cola name and logo above it. I immediately went to the general manager's office and told him he had to take Pepsi-Cola down and put Coca-Cola up right away. Our major sponsor is Coca-Cola. We can't have Pepsi all over the place – we need Coca-Cola!

He said he couldn't do that, but if he could get Coca-Cola as his exclusive soft drink he would do it. I asked how many soft drinks he sold daily. Can you believe around 40,000 per day? I immediately called Walter Dunn at Coca Cola and told him the good news about their volume. I asked how much it would cost the hotel to take Pepsi out and put in Coca-Cola, and how long it would take.

Here is a lesson in common sense business. Mr. Dunn said that the Coca-Cola bottler can be there within one hour and exchange all equipment, logos, etc., by five o'clock that day for free, and give the hotel the first month free.

Let's see, 40,000 Coca-Cola brand products per day being consumed, and marquee signage to a network sports program. Dominique Wilkens (Atlanta) was our Official NBA Star Commissioner, and ninety-six cities were all vying to be on the finale show of the Coca-Cola Coup de Hoop three-on-three Basketball Championships. This was a slam dunk for the hotel – and me.

There was even a bonus for my company for creating the conversion of this unique property from Pepsi to Coca-Cola. Made sense to me since the hotel was averaging 40,000 soft drinks, water, etc., per day. Coca-Cola would have an exclusive on all non-alcoholic liquid drinks. That is a very healthy daily financial gain for any company including a major one like Coca-Cola.

Everyone was excited and happy. The hotel gave me a large check because Coke gave them the first month free. Did we dodge a bullet and wake up in clover? It was truly a great day. Renny was on a roll!

Just when you think you can do no wrong is when you should not get cocky and make sure all I's are dotted and all T's are crossed. Or in other words, instead of slapping yourself on the back, look carefully at what's in front of you, and make the best of it. At the same time, make sure you are preserving what you have while building a better future on what seems like a success.

One of the most exciting aspects of this second year event with the Coca-Cola triumph over Pepsi-Cola and the additional time on network television was the fact that my daughter would sing the national anthem on network television at the age of twelve-years-old. Remember, I was in the music business representing and promoting some of the biggest stars, in the world. My daughter can sing!

I was excited on game day like I always am for one of my events, but this time I was nervous that my daughter would pull off one of the toughest songs to sing in the world, our national anthem!

The guys on the television crew told me to relax. she'll be fine as I checked with her for the fiftieth time. "Are you ok?"

Boy was I nervous. I knew she could do it. We had packed stands with over 4,000 spectators. CBS Cameras were everywhere along with nervous amateur basketball players, hotel execs were getting their moment on the screen on a hot day in Vegas.

Just before going to center court in 112 degree desert heat, a kind young lady put some suntan protective lotion on my daughter so she wouldn't get burned. She told me what she had done and I thanked her and chastised myself inwardly because I had not thought to do that. As a single parent to three youngsters, I should have thought of sunscreen.

Needless to say my daughter was awesome. The event went great, and within one hour the location was almost back to normal. Sineta (my daughter) and I were going to drive back to Thousand Oaks California. My daughter told me she didn't feel well. All the ringside doctors, including me, chalked it up to nerves and the incredible response from the audience.

Especially since she couldn't tell me exactly what was bothering her. We began the drive back to California, laughing and joking about the great time we had. The exciting response from the crowd etc. After we crossed over into California, Sineta told me her face felt funny. It did look a little puffy, but we both chalked it up to desert sunburn. Then, she felt like her face was beginning to swell.

I didn't want to panic because we were now about thirty minutes from home. I could literally see her face beginning to swell. Fifteen minutes from home, twelve minutes from the hospital and now it's really swelling up. I'm scared to death.

What if she was stung by poisonous bug or something while in the desert?

Nine minutes to home, six to emergency room, left turn, right turn. Two blocks, another turn and then into the Emergency Room parking lot. I don't even think I locked the doors. Nothing and no one came before my only daughter and youngest child. In the emergency room I was recognized by one of the supervisors as "Somebody Special" and they whisked us into a room followed by a doctor within a few minutes.

The doctor asked if my daughter had used any suntan lotion while in Vegas and I said yes. He wanted to know if it contained Paba? Neither of us had an answer so I ran out to the car and found the bottle and ran back inside.

Yes, it had Paba, so now what? We ended up with a few simple tests, a prescription with a few free days of medication. We also had a big hospital, doctor and prescription bill as well as a daughter with a towel over her head so no one will see her,

I know what my beautiful daughter looks like, and right now it's horrific, like something out of a "B" monster movie. Here is where you face an important reality check and recognition as a parent, especially single parents. This is my child, and I love her. Right now, her well-being, and life is in someone else's hands. I don't have a solution to her problem except to be calm, keep her calm, and promise it's going to be alright. No matter what!

Four years later at sixteen, my daughter sang the national anthem at a Miami Dolphins game and performed in front of a sold out concert featuring Luther Vandross. She also, shortly after that, made it into the top twelve on American Idol.

Always remember there is nothing more important and greater than your children. At the same time, taking care of them demands concentration and a willingness to maximize every intelligence factor you have to perform at your peak as close to 100% of the time as is possible.

When someone asks me what was the most difficult event and best results I ever produced I tell them "my children." The funny part about that is, I had absolutely no control over the delivery or the outcome. I had to accept whatever was given to me and work like crazy to make the best, provide the best, and most of all teach them to be the best they can be. Then let them forge the trail with the only interruption being a love shove in the right direction from time to time when they become adults!

Sometimes living a nightmare but staying positive can lead you to the best times of your life. I lost millions in the Hugo disaster, yet I cherish these times as some of the most invigorating times of my life. Positivity always wins.

## Children First, Money Second

Sometimes the truth and facts of life may cause you to have to eliminate things in your life for the perseverance of your family. You may see dollars, promotions, and other fine opportunities as the result. But regardless of all of that, nothing is more important than the health and safety of your family.

I was a single parent for many years. Kelly was my oldest child at home and sometimes the only one with me. I had raised him by myself from eighteen-months to twenty-one-years old.

I remember my son going to one of my concerts and on the drive home he asked me, "Dad, do you want me to be a drug addict?"

I of course said, "No." In my entire life I had never had even a few hits on a joint. When I asked Kelly why he asked, he told me that he could have had enough illegal drugs at my concert that night to last a lifetime.

He said, "Dad, it was real bad and I'm sure I got a contact high just being around it."

I spent about ten minutes explaining that drug usage is a byproduct of the concerts I produce even though I don't do drugs myself. Fortunately he did not become a drug user nor fan of drugs.

As a matter of fact, he even stopped me from smoking cigarettes and made me over $300,000. But that's another story

to be told a little later. First the concert situation. My son Kelly
has a very strong mind and utilizes this power to the max.

As a father you always try to maximize the positive and
minimize or eliminate the negative. This was a huge problem
and I had to deal with it right away. My son had challenged me
on whether or not I supported drug use by young people.

There was only one answer. The next day I ceased to co-own
the P-Funk tour. But before all that happened, the P-Funk tour
had "sold out" the largest venues all over the U.S. It began on
August 15, 1978, probably the biggest financial year of my life.

The first P-Funk performance was at Soldiers Field in Chicago.
Along with Abe Thompson (Sales Executive at WVON Radio),
and Tom Joyner (all night disc jockey at WJPC) the Johnson
Publishing (Ebony magazine) owned radio station, we mounted
the greatest promotion ever created and executed in the history
of black concerts. Soldiers Field was the location and the heat
was unbelievable.

Pre-event promotion began three months from the event. Ticket
prices were set at fifty-five dollars with an expected audience
of 65,000 live bodies. We filled the market with "give-aways"
of about 2,000 tickets (saved thousands on advertising).

We did promotions in schools, other concerts, retail outlets,
adult organizations, record stores, parades, concerts, every
nightclub, basketball/football/baseball game, private parties
and record hops, stories and bios in local newspapers, radio and
television.

No stone was left unturned. We even promised a donation of
one dollar per person to the United Negro College Fund and
contacted every black college within five nearby states, and
sent fliers to every black college cause.

We were scheduled (if successful), to take this tour to just
about every state. It was a job for hundreds; it was completed

by three persons. It was the kick-off to the most successful black artist tour in history for five consecutive years. Actually we missed our forecast by 20,000 people and ended up with 89,000 sold tickets.

I walked away from all this in order to keep my son from becoming involved with drugs. He knew that, and so did I. But I was also aware of other opportunities already standing by to take place - and they did.

**Reinventing Yourself**

Too often many people, after they turn fifty, feel everything worthwhile in life is over. Boy, do they not know the real truth. Positive thoughts and actions will win you all kinds of personal rewards and joy, regardless of your age.

Staying positive after fifty is extremely important. Being over fifty doesn't make you ancient, it just makes you "aware" and with a history and knowledge that cannot be compared to young adults.

There is much an eighteen-year-old can learn from you. They can increase their status by listening to you. Equally important is to listen to your heart and mind, believe in yourself, and do not give up!

After the Screen Actors Guild strike, my acting career began to move in a positive direction. I was playing McMurphy (the lead character) on stage for two years in "One Flew over the Cuckoo's Nest." It was awesome being crazy on stage where the audience never knew what I might do and say on any given evening.

Don't get me wrong. I followed the script ninety-nine percent to the letter, but each night a different McMurphy took the stage. It was just different enough for me to know in my private sanctum playing a crazy man.

Reviews were great. We stayed "sold out" and I had finally achieved a life's goal - to be able to guide a play by being the lead character with the most outstanding group of actors I ever met. They were incredible as they pushed me to my best night every night. I remember one evening sitting in the dressing room, dripping wet from the sheer exhaustion of the effort put out.

It wasn't until we had four or five shows completed that the producer called me into his office and showed me a letter from the author of the play. The letter acknowledged Renny Roker as the first African-American approved (as far as he knew) to play the lead role of McMurphy in "Cuckoo's Nest." When I asked the producer, he said he received the letter three days prior to opening night.

Each actor had opportunities to invite casting directors, directors, and producers. I invited at least 200 people if not more. Most of them came. As a result, I was working at every studio in town, and doing the play on weekends. Somehow you never get tired when you are happy, and I was real happy!

By this time I had amassed a number of "firsts" and took the time to try to understand exactly what that meant. Was it special or should I have been asking, "Why me?" and "Why only me?" I wasn't suffering from any delusions, thinking I was better than the plethora of great black talent, executives, voices, etc., on the market.

I was very fortunate and I realized that a man I would no longer be able to thank (Nat "King" Cole) was gone. He'd made a phone call to Otto Preminger that launched my acting career.

In 1974, I starred in a motion picture called "Johnny Tough" which was written, produced and directed by Horace Jackson. It was a "G" rated black film about a middle class black family so wrapped up in their own good fortune that they had forsaken their only child who was not only feeling left out, he had begun to act out.

While making the movie, we ran out of money a little more than halfway through production. Twentieth Century Fox gave us $75,000 to complete the film. We gave them first right of refusal. By that time, Horace had made me a co-producer on the film and we worked night and day.

Horace was without a doubt the most complete film maker I ever knew. He had me working with him in the edit room and behind the scenes. But the responsibility I loved the most was the promotion of the movie. I was ready to step up to the table.

We finished the film and as promised took it to Twentieth Century Fox to review and distribute or send us on our way. At the time of this movie, most black films were either street comedies or full of sex, drugs and violence.

Twentieth screened the film at least twenty times. After exhausting every decision maker, they declared our movie a great film however, not sellable without drugs, sex and fighting. Amazing! But they made their contribution to complete the film a gift to us with their best wishes.

What happened next was incredible. Horace, I, and a few others went to Atlanta, Georgia. We promoted the movie in every school in the city. We invited the captains of every athletic team, top cheerleaders from every school, top students from every school and the most popular kids in each grade level from every school. Oh yes, and we even invited some popular teachers too.

Screening was at the Fox Theater, which held about 2,500 people. We rented the theater for our screening and booked the theater to carry the film "four walled," renting the whole theater for one movie.

When the theater manager saw the number of patrons coming with free-entry passes, plus the plethora of press, he proclaimed that we just gave away all the tickets we would have sold.

What followed was the most incredible box office numbers in Atlanta history. We sold out eighteen successive weekends at the Fox Theater, breaking all attendance records (at that time) at the theater. We made a deal with Dimension Pictures, to distribute our film, with a major opening in New York and other cities.

We had a family film in four theaters on 42nd Street in New York, which were not known for family entertainment. We sold out all showings at each theater. When it was all over, we grossed more than forty million dollars, an equivalent in today's box office admission prices over $300 million dollars in box office receipts. "Johnny Tough" was the first black film to reach number one in Daily Variety Box Office tallies in the U.S.

Sometimes, being the first to accomplish something significant is not always the best place to be. This is especially true when there is an opportunity to see what can be done and then improve on it. But there I was once more, the first, or part of the team that was first to reach number one in Daily Variety Box Office receipts, and a hit movie.

I still think back on the days of stealing shots because we couldn't afford permits, using everyone's houses and sneaking into classrooms and playgrounds on the weekends, using each other's homes for our residences in the film, and editing from 8:00pm till the next morning non-stop.

I don't know where Horace Jackson is anymore and can't seem to find him. Horace is an incredible film maker who never received the recognition he deserved. I feel honored to have worked with and partnered with him in the two films we produced together.

Thought - One thing for sure is that life is never over till you say it's over. There are so many people running around retired from life not job, retired from joy and friends, just because they turned fifty or over. I have discovered that life after fifty is awesome, forgiving, exciting, calm and peaceful yet full of joy and happiness. It's also the best time to reinvent yourself without caring what people think! This is your time to explore, create and live as though there is no tomorrow just today.

## It Pays to Have History

No one remembers the feats you have accomplished. So simply undertake new deeds. Go out and sell yourself all over again, except this time you have history, knowledge, and an anti-explosion insurance called "experience."

Positivity can carry anything forward, provided you keep the faith in your experience, renewed positive energy in your heart, and your refusal to accept the negative while you are still breathing. It really does pay to have knowledge of yesterday. If you do, for sure you will understand and accept the positives of tomorrow.

When I think of it, my life has included coaching little league baseball, basketball, soccer junior teams and/or organizations in golf, BMX, track, radio announcer, producer of television programs, motion pictures, child tap dancer, choir singer, destruction of a school, triathlon, three on three basketball, junior golf, Harlem Globetrotters, voice-overs, radio and television, actor television, documentaries, motion picture, promoter of concerts to millions of attendees, radio announcer, host, amateur athlete, top student from first grade to college, father, grandfather, great grandfather, married too many times, first African-American to produce their own sports special series for ABC, \CBS, NBC, ESPN, Turner, & Golf Channel.

So what does someone my age pursue? Someone who is as fit as most fit men in their forties? You create the greatest and most unique events in the world for all to see and only the privileged to participate. You create a youth sports spectacular, a global, most difficult marathon, a global after school homework assistance program, and Global BMX Championship.

If you are going to go out with a true tribute to your past, you might as well incorporate all your former activities into the present and or near future. In that manner there is no question who you were and who you still are. So many have ridden into the sunset with a huge clap of thunder created by their intense accomplishments.

The future is now, the past is behind us and there is no time like the present to prepare. So here goes:

There have been moments in my life where very profound statements or actions have taken place to have a distinct impact on me and others around me.

I remember at one point in securing spokesperson or acting gigs for commercial products, I found a groove that was working great for me in securing jobs. I had more than twenty national commercials running at one time. Sometimes, I would walk into an interviewing lounge area with many other actors and you could hear the groan. The actors immediately began thinking I would get the contract.

It was a remarkable period and I do believe a great deal had to do with how I felt about myself. I'm not ego tripping, or self-centered, just comfortable with myself, in love with life and contented.

What more could I ask for? I was happy, my son was happy. I would soon be heading out on the road with my son to promote a movie called "Johnny Tough" in which I had the lead role. As a single parent, I was taking my son with me. We spent that summer on the road having a great time. We ate out or had room service every day as we traveled from city to city. It was great and I loved it.

I had six scholarships to college when I graduated from Christiansted High School on St. Croix, Virgin Islands. I didn't have the airfare to the cities, plus the extra dollars it would cost me, so I took a scholarship from Inter American University in San German, Puerto Rico. I loved it.

An incredible university: two things will always stand out in my mind. The first was my history professor (an older woman) Dr. Casby. On our first day of class she told everyone, "Tell me the story, tell me what happened, and if you don't know the exact date but you know exactly what happened that's most important."

I fell in love with this elderly woman immediately. This was my kind of class - "Tell me the story." I loved college! My Spanish was weak but with so many beautiful girls on campus I learned this romantic language very quickly!

I was young, sixteen-years-old in college and experiencing being away from family for the first time. Most people around me spoke another language. So, I learned the language, had a great time with all the Spanish students, and discovered a new life, girlfriends and the importance of knowing what you're talking about.

This was the beginning of "Renny the story-teller" and the most important ride of my life in three-and-a-half years, with over twenty credits each semester.

Every year in college I would go back to St. Croix and my radio program. The feeling of being at home again was wonderful. Another thing became very apparent to me: No matter where you are it's important to have a place you can call home.

Neither my grandmother nor grandfather ever took a pill in their lives. Natural herbs and plants were their medicine. From mint tea to the leaves of the Soursop fruit which was as healing as Nyquil without any drugs or other man-made elements.

They bought themselves out of slavery for very little money, invested in land, built a home, and were much respected in St. Croix.

All of this played a key role in my activities. Some kept me grounded, but much of it sent me on a trip that would include more than seventy countries around the world. I learned humility without power, knowledge to be used when needed, not flaunted, and respect for women (wow, that was a big one!). Oh yes, and using common sense.

Most times it was not the obvious that made me successful. Those unique moments that lead to innovative ideas I acted on which brought me the most success. Most of those were the result of everyday events, people that I met, and things I observed. I have the gift of seeing things for what could be. In other words – I look at the world through the eyes of positivity.

I have to say that I started as a happy youngster. I had a good family and a wonderful childhood. There wasn't a lot of drama at home. There weren't any alcoholics, wife beaters, or child abuse. We were "broke as skunks", as my father would say. Looking back, maybe that contributed to my ability to innovate.

I remember my first three-wheel bike had a missing pedal. Only the rod held the pedal. There was a steep hill in my neighborhood. It scared me to look at it, nonetheless to attempt to ride it. I went down it anyway. I had to. My sister, Denise did it. You see, Denise is a year younger than me.

We were both very competitive. Anything she did, of course, I had to do it better. In retrospect, we pushed each other to excellence. It is likely that we would never have achieved as much as we did without that fierce competition.

Denise and I challenged each other in reading, spelling, math, history, geography and just about anything else we had available; Monopoly, Fish (card game), book reading. By the ages of five and six, respectively, my sister and I read just about every book in the house.

We were both straight "A" students in school except for conduct. I was notorious for getting a "D" with a big red circle around it suggesting that my behavior was very bad. I wanted to talk all the time. Sometimes the teacher would begin explaining items from books we were about to read. Often I had already read the book and was anxious to tell the class all about it.

I was never a great athlete, but I tried just about all of them available; football, basketball, baseball, track and field. I even tried my hand at Golden Gloves boxing as a teenager. In about my fifth or sixth match, I was beat up so bad I never returned. I never understood the excitement about boxing anyway. I appreciated what I learned. Boxing taught me how to protect myself. Even better, I got a reputation as a boxer and so, not too many people bothered with me.

I was about four years old when my family moved from the Bronx "Ghetto" to the quiet suburbs of St. Albans, Queens, New York. My father insisted we move after he found a rat in my bathtub.

While in the Bronx, the entire family lived in a small two bedroom apartment. There were three children and two adults in the small space. We lived on the third floor. There were no elevators and no air conditioning.

The smell of urine was a constant in the hallways. Trash always sat on the steps, as well as roaches and rats in all of the walls. While both of my parents had high school degrees, they could not find employment that would afford them to move out.

That rat in the tub probably had the most profound impact on my childhood. In some strange twist of fate, I am grateful for that rat. As fast as that rat fell into the tub, my dad grabbed me out. He told me, my mother, my sister and older brother to get dressed. He announced, "We are moving to Long Island".

Actually we moved to St. Albans, Queens. Back in the forties and coming from the Bronx, it looked like Long Island. There were nice brick homes, green grass, and fruit trees in every backyard. We had wooded areas where kids (including me) could pretend to be cowboys and Indians. We were explorers with sling shots, instead of real guns. We used our imagination to create all sorts of games and opportunities to explore.

Our backyard sported a peach, apple and pear tree, along with a grape vine. My mom canned the fruit so we had it all year long. She baked pies and fruit cakes. She also made fruit drinks. My mom knew how to get the most of what we had.

We had lots of grass which my brother and I mowed weekly. When we weren't mowing, my sister would join us in weeding, sweeping, painting or cleaning. We had to. My father would wake us every Saturday morning. He would tell us that he didn't work as hard as he did to have the worst looking yard in the neighborhood. I truly lived a storybook childhood.

At age twelve, I considered myself an incredible woman's man. This was funny since I had never actually been close to a girl, nonetheless kissed one. Most of my friends were older, so I had to hold my own. I remember going to a party. It was a Slow Dance Party (known at the time as a "Grind").

I was anxious to be close to a girl. I knew there would be lots of them there. And there were.

I found myself overwhelmed with the music and the girls. I was on a direct flight to heaven. It was shortly after that when I lost my virginity. Fortunately, we moved shortly after that to the island of St. Croix in the U.S. Virgin Islands.

My dad, who had worked three jobs (twenty-four hours) per day for a few years, was experiencing heart problems. To give him the much deserved and needed rest, my parents moved us to my grandparents' home.

I have fond memories of my time there. In fact, I remember my teachers. They really cared about the students. It was a nice reminder of my kindergarten teacher in St. Albans, Queens, Mrs. Paterson.

Before I left New York, I had become an ardent listener to the black radio stations with D.J.'s like Jocko, Dr. Jive and Allen Freed (he was Caucasian). I loved the music. I especially loved when they played the hit songs of my older brother Wally and his group The Heartbeats. They had six consecutive million plus selling records. I was his biggest fan.

Much to my delight, the unthinkable took place in this peaceful paradise. The local radio station held a teenage disc jockey contest. The winner would get their own Saturday radio show. This was the only radio station on St. Croix.

There was no television and no movie theatre to speak of. This was a 10,000 Clear Channel wattage station sitting on the east coast at the ocean. There was nothing in its path, only the ocean and eastern sea coast. The signal could run up the entire east coast and be heard in many coastal cities, including New York and Bermuda.

This was an opportunity I could not pass on. I "stole" the name, Dr. Jive, from my New York radio listening days. I called myself, Renny "Dr. Jive" Roker. I then incorporated all of the "tricks" used by the New York DJs. I got the attention of the judges, the local youth and adults. I won the contest and went on to host my own show. Not too bad for a fourteen-year-old.

When I think about it, the Renny "Dr. Jive" Roker show was the real beginning of my career in the entertainment industry. My Saturday program was going great. Soon after I started, my counterpart at the radio station in St. Thomas joined me in an evening program. We had a simulcast of the two stations with the two teenager disc jockeys; Renny "Dr Jive" Roker and Addie Ottley. We did it all and called it the The Tri-Island Ballroom.

We got calls and requests from just about every island in the Caribbean, and as far away as New York, and other eastern cities. The success of our Saturday evening program and week night programs was recognized by advertisers, as well as the families in the Caribbean.

For a young man, the radio show made a big impact on my personal life. The station was only a three minute walk away from the beach, actually down a slight hill. So on those many weekends, I would simply play the entire side of an album so that I could run down to the beach.

I got it down to an art. I could get back to the studio before the record finished. There were lots of beautiful girls on the beach listening to the "Dr. Jive" show. Sometimes there were hundreds of kids (schoolmates) on the beach, listening to my show. I was the local celebrity.

It was about this time in my life that I started to have a vision. While I was still young and I wasn't sure how I was going to achieve it, I believed in it. I wanted to be part of the entertainment industry. This was funny for a young man that did not drink, do drugs or enjoy wild crazy parties. It was a crazy time in that industry. But I wanted a part of it.

I was ready to take on the long hours, constant phone calls and letters. I learned from my brother who was already making a name for himself that it was about communications and communicating. It was the way you got things done.

After college I had the opportunity to join my brother as his assistant in promoting records. Back then you got in the car, train or plane and you went from city to city, radio station to radio station, and occasionally you even found a few guys on television like Dick Clark, or unique jocks like John R. who was the all night guy on a 50,000 watt Clear Channel station out of Nashville Tenn.

John R. attracted listeners in at least fifty percent of U.S. homes including New York. His station WLAC was 50,000 watts Clear Channel, which had listeners in more than 30 States.

## Enter Nat "King" Cole

I'll never forget my first road trip for Nat "King" Cole's label, K.C. Records. I was promoting a Barbara McNair record and I had heard that the jocks in Chicago liked her and really liked Mr. Cole. My brother, who was already a renowned and respected record promoter, gave me the names and stations I had to see, and communicate with. I was very excited because one, I had never been to Chicago, and two, these guys (outside of New York jocks) were the most powerful in radio at that time.

I was only making $75 per week and my expense budget was quite small, so I picked a hotel close to downtown Chicago and close to a major post office. I had a vision that this would be a very successful trip.

I went to my first radio station and the disc jockey invited me into the studio with him (now that's progress I thought). He asked me to have a seat where he could see me and talk to me. He told me how many years he had been on radio (more than I had been on this earth), and all the major celebrities he had met etc.

Then he asked me how much money did I bring for him to play my record? I sat there in shock, but told the truth. I had no money for him. He looked at me real hard. "You work for the richest black entertainer in the world, and you come to me with no money? Are you crazy?" He took my records and broke them right in front of me on the edge of his desk.

When the record he was playing finished, he opened his microphone and said, "I have a record promotion man representing one of the biggest and greatest stars in the world, and he came to me with no money! What should I do? Make it or break it?"

"I'll answer my own question, I will break it, that's what I'll do!" He proceeded to break my records into little bitty pieces then threw them at me, as he yelled, "Don't ever come back here to Chicago begging!"

Then he took out a gun and a large dagger and put them on the console in between us. He looked me dead in the eyes and said "And don't you move from that chair, even if you got to pee, pee in your pants."

I was scared to death. This was my first road trip and my first face to face with a very popular D.J. and it was not going well at all.

When the record he was playing stopped he asked me where I was staying. I told him and he laughed at me. "Well, you don't stay there any longer. When I get off the air, Rodney and I are going to check you out of that flea bag hotel and check you into the Sheraton in downtown Chicago."

"If you want our help you got to impress us, and host us to a big dinner and drinks." The cash register in my head reminded me that I had called the Sheraton and one night there was more than my entire budget, but before I could say something he said "I'm calling Rodney (E Rodney Jones, another very powerful disc jockey) and tell him to book a suite in your name and order about twelve bottles of liquor for your party."

What party? *This is getting worse*, I thought. The hotel small rooms were too expensive and a suite with twelve bottles of liquor was more than my annual salary. What am I going to tell my boss and Mr. Cole?

Now I did have to go to the bathroom. Thank God his show was ending. He must have known what was going on and said "If you got to go to the bathroom go ahead." Another big D.J. was walking into the studio to do his shift. He said "Are you Renny, Nat "King" Cole's promo man?"

All I could do was nod yes. "Great! I'm looking forward to attending your party tonight at the Sheraton, downtown. What's your suite number?"

I told him I hadn't checked in as yet. "That's ok. The guys will let me know," he said. "Looks like about twenty-five guys plus a bunch of ladies are coming."

*Oh my God. I'm cooked, fired, and probably on my way to jail for non-payment of my hotel suite, liquor and whatever else they have in store for me.*

"Oh, and I hear you've ordered filet mignon for each of us and great deserts, is that true?"

*Oh my God this is getting worse by the minute,* I thought.

At that time Rodney entered the studio. He and Richard drove me over to my low budget hotel, had me pay for the evening I wouldn't stay there, then drove me to the Sheraton Downtown Chicago.

What a hotel! It was beautiful, but difficult for me to appreciate because all I could see was dollar signs, going to jail for non-payment of my bill and who knows what else.

We were now at the front desk as the three of us approached, a lovely lady said, "You must be Mr. Roker?"

I thought, *How did she know that?*

"We have your suite ready and took the liberty to decorate it for your party tonight. I added it to your bill already, but if you don't want it we can get rid of it for you before the party."

Both guys looked at me as I squeaked out, "No that's ok you can leave it there." Both men smiled and nodded their approval. We went up to the suite and I almost passed out.

It was on the top floor. You could see the lights of Chicago just coming on. It was breathtaking, but who was going to pay for this? I just knew that tomorrow I would be in jail.

It looked like every disc jockey in Chicago attended my party. It was unbelievable. I met every power broker in music in Chicago that night. I was king, but I knew by morning I would be a jailbird in the local jail.

Deep down inside me there was a feeling that everything was going to be ok! Somehow I was feeling positive and decided to go along with whatever was going to happen. Despite that feeling, I was still nervous.

Rodney kept asking me if I was having a good time. I said yes, but I knew he knew what I was thinking. This was going to turn into a catastrophe. The next morning, with half the crowd still in the suite asleep on couches and the other two bedrooms in the suite (yes it was a three bedroom suite with two pull out sofas from the couches), I called my office in New York.

They were worried about me because I had checked out of the hotel I said I was staying at. I remembered telling a lie about why I moved out but knew I was in trouble, big trouble.

One thing for sure, the party was a huge success. Everyone said they would play the new Barbra McNair record on Mr. Cole's label. Everyone said it would be a big hit within two weeks, and that if I held these kinds of parties across the country it would be number one on the charts within three weeks.

All I could think of was that the only numbers I would see would be the numbers on my prison uniform. This was great in some ways but desperately too close to a bonafide jail term for the promotion man (me!), and a lot of bad press for my boss Nat "King" Cole.

When I got downstairs to discuss checking out (how was I going to do that?) the front desk clerk congratulated me for extending my stay two days. Oh no. I knew I was in trouble for one night, but three nights?

Now I know I'm going to jail. Why are these guys doing this to me? Why are they trying to get me fired and in jail too? I went back up to my room and found the room filled with small portable tables with coffee, bagels, eggs, bacon, sausage, milk, juice, and other goodies.

Oh my God, they are going to throw the key! Another night of partying, with lots of bottles of booze, and party favors. Everyone loved me, and for a moment I even felt good until one guy, half-drunk, walked up to me and asked, "How many thousands of dollars did this cost"?

I responded, "Not too many," as I thought about how many years behind bars I would see.

I finally called my brother and told him what was happening, and he told me his famous line, "Don't panic, it will work itself out."

I was past panicking. I was scared to death. The party continued, except now radio personalities from Milwaukee and surrounding states and cities joined in and we had an incredible multi-city and states party. The party had hit every city and state in the country by now and we even had disc jockeys from California and New York attending the third and final evening.

My phone in the hotel was ringing off the hook with radio announcers calling to confirm the party from all over the U.S. I was very happy, but knew I was facing a long jail term when they handed me my bill and I tell them that I have no money, just a plane ticket to get home, if I get to go home.

The last night was incredible. Radio stars from around the country, lots of positive PR that upgraded my status in the industry, as well as my brother's. It was really great. By this time Jack Gale, Mr. Cole's partner had heard about the parties and all the radio disc jockeys that attended. He understood the significance of this kind of support and wanted to know how was I going to pay for it, because it wasn't in his budget.

That answered my question. Was Jack going to pay for this, knowing how big this had become? I was definitely in trouble. My thoughts were that I would be called a huge success that went to jail.

Even with pending jail time I was excited. Thanks to my brother and the Chicago disc-jockeys, the whole country knew about our huge successful party. The next morning three of the Chicago radio personalities said they would meet me and give me a ride to the airport.

*"Oh no,"* I thought. I had not changed my ticket. I dressed and packed and went downstairs to face the music. When I walked up to the front desk the lady behind the desk was all smiles. She wanted to know if I enjoyed my stay and congratulated me in introducing so many influential people from around the country to their hotel.

Wow. Not what I expected. Then the incredible, "Mr Roker, when you return to Chicago, I've been authorized to provide you with a suite for three days on the hotel."

What's next? "Have a safe trip home and thank you for the kind manner in which you rewarded our staff members. We all love you here at the Sheraton. Don't be long in returning," she said with a big smile.

A funny thing happened then. Instead of asking for payment, she gave me a copy of my receipt and turned to go to another guest leaving me standing there waiting for something to happen.

I went back up to my room, got my bag, and went downstairs. Five of the Chicago disc jockeys met me at front desk. They took my bag and handed me a new plane ticket. They thanked me for the best weekend they ever had in their lives.

The next thing that happened was unbelievable; I broke down and cried like a baby. These guys had paid for the entire weekend. When I asked them why, they said because they believed in me and that I could become the first man of color to become the first top executive in the music industry at a Major Label. Now the tears really started going crazy. These guys, old enough to be my dad, had just endorsed me in their own way. This was incredible and awesome all at the same time.

I did become the first African-American executive at a major multi-million dollar record company. But that's another story.

As you can see, I've experienced quite a bit in my life. Many would be astounded at what I've been able to accomplish. Yet I still find that my past accomplishments don't necessarily carry much weight and I must re-establish myself with new undertakings.

How? I remain positive and optimistic that I will be able to move forward with whatever I decide to set my mind to. Does this mean I won't run into roadblocks? Absolutely not. My history tells me to stay positive, believe in myself, and keep on keepin' on…

# Nat "King" Cole's Last Hit Record

No matter how far down in the pecking order of your job you might think you are, always remember that you are there for an important reason. Regardless of what that reason is, you and only you are responsible for making it work to the expectations of your boss and company.  You also should find ways to exceed everyone's expectations by raising the bar to higher levels. Often, this will result in your receiving increased pay or position or even both.  More importantly, it will make you proud and excited!

Positivity does work. Sometimes having a vision will set your mind in the right direction. A vision needs fuel for action. That is your job, to set yourself in motion and follow your positive path. Who knows where you will end up!

My first job in the music business was as a promotion/ publishing rep for Nat "King" Cole working out of his partners' office (Jack and Ada Gayle) on the East Side (55<sup>th</sup> St.) of New York. Prior to that, after college in Puerto Rico, I spent a great deal of time learning the business from my brother and Al Sears at their music publishing, record promotion, and record producing office. Seemed like all of the music business leaders were in and out of that office at some point during each week.

I also met a man named Clarence Avant who managed two of the biggest names in jazz, Wes Montgomery and Jimmy Smith. When I met him he had just signed his artist Jimmy Smith, the first one million dollar contract for a jazz artist in the music business. Mr. Avant also represented several Presidents

including John F. Kennedy as their minority peoples'
representative.

My first job at Mr. Cole's office was to get a Nat "King" Cole
published song on Jimmy Smith's first album on his new label.
Of course, I went to Mr. Avant. His first question was, "Is this
going to help you in your job?"

Of course (and it was true), I said yes!

He said ok, but he wanted a song on Mr. Cole's next album.
This was great! Eighteen-years-old, fresh out of college, and
I'm wheeling and dealing with the big guys. Then the same
thing happened with my brother. He got a song on Mr. Cole's
album and I got a song on one of his artist's album.

The truth was, no one knew when the next Nat "King" Cole
album would come out. He needed a hit song in order to really
have a big selling album. The label, as well as Jack and Ada,
wanted him to record a Rock n' Roll song. I knew this was the
wrong thing for Mr. Cole. I also knew that he needed a hit
record in order to even get a new album.

I had a vision! I had my own marching orders! Go find Mr.
Cole a hit song. One day I was sitting at my desk and listening
to songs that came in. There was one song that I kept going
back to listen to. No one in Mr. Cole's office liked the song,
but I knew it would be perfect for him and possibly a big hit.

Of course, this was before CD's, DVD's, and even email, so I
put the song into the mail with a note.

*Dear Mr. Cole. I know you are searching for the right song
and I know that Capitol Records and Jack and Ada want you to
record a Rock-n-Roll song, but you are not a Rock-n-Roll artist
and you don't have to be one. Please listen to this song,
"Ramblin Rose." This will be a big hit for you.*

I knew I was crossing the line, but I had a vision of how to make this record a big hit. I convinced Jack and Ada and Capital Records executives to invite the top R&B disc jockeys to see Mr. Cole perform at the Copa Cabana in New York and the Latin Casino in Cherry Hill New Jersey.

I just knew that if I could get "Jocko", Georgie Woods, Dr Jive, the guys in Baltimore, WSID/Washington D.C. WOL, and Chicago's Rodney Jones and Al Benson, and others to play Mr. Cole's new recording, I would become one of the most popular and respected record promotion men in the country.

Mr. Cole's last hit was a few years ago at this time. His style was being usurped by The Beatles and several others now in the limelight. I began by calling Mr. Cole in California which was a no-no for me in those days, but I did it anyway.

"Mr. Cole," I said, "I'm sorry to bother you, but I sent you a song, Ramblin Rose, which I think could be your next big hit."

He thanked me and said Jack and Ada and Capital wants me to do a Rock n' Roll song. I then stepped over the line by saying, "Mr. Cole, you are not a Rock n' Roll singer. You are better, much better than that. You are one of the finest voices in the world."

Mr. Cole asked me if I staked my job on this song. Time to really follow my vision. I said it.

"I bet my job on this song."

Mr. Cole said, "Ok. I'll do it, but it will be on the "B" side and you will have to get the disc jockeys to play your side."

I invited all the top disc jockeys in the country to see Mr. Cole sing in Philadelphia. I had the hottest jocks in the city come to the event. One talked me into letting him go to the Copa with his girlfriend, and then his wife to the Latin Casino in New Jersey (10 minutes from Philadelphia).

All of the disc jockeys loved their evening with Mr. Cole's
incredible song singing style. It was time for the song to be
released. It was on the same week Capitol Records was
bringing the Beatles to the U.S.

The last thing that was on their mind was Mr. Cole's latest
record. That was great for me because it gave me at least two
weeks to do something. Actually, I spent six consecutive weeks
on the road refusing to return home until the job was
completed.

My first stop was Philadelphia. The famous disc jockey who
took his girlfriend to one and his wife to the other refused to
play Mr. Cole's record. He didn't play that kind of music, but
he loved the music of Mr. Cole.

I threatened to call his wife and did so right in front of him
feigning to forget which show she attended. He made me hang
up the phone and played the record. Every phone in the studio
lit up with praises for the new Nat "King" Cole hit record.

He played that record about six times and the phone kept
ringing for more! "Play it again," they all said.

By the time my six week trip was up, Mr. Cole's record was in
the top twenty in the country, heading for the number one slot.
I had a vision and made that vision come true.

I was now truly a "real" promotion executive in the music
business, and Mr. Cole was my hero. The opportunity to
become recognized by the music industry was amazing.

Soon after this great hit made it to the top of the charts, Mr.
Cole called me on the phone. He told me he wanted to meet
with me. I was elated. He told me he heard I was in off
Broadway stage plays as an actor (true), and he was going to
let me go.

I wanted to cry. I told him I would cease acting immediately. He said, "No way. It's time for you to move on, so I'm introducing you to Otto Preminger (Paramount Pictures) to help you with acting jobs. I will introduce you to Al Bennett President/Owner Liberty Records in Los Angeles. You'll become the first (Negro) African American executive in the music business."

This was a very strange kind of firing. He reminded me that I had been involved in off Broadway plays in New York and obviously enjoyed acting. He stated I should pursue acting if I really enjoyed it as long as I did not quit my "day job" after my first acting job.

One day after meeting Otto Preminger, I was in the Gomer Pyle Show, and later that week signed a contract to be a recurring regular on the show. I ended up in twenty-nine episodes of Gomer Pyle. I also had a bit role in Preminger's next film "Skidoo" which had Jackie Gleason, George Raft, and many other big stars.

I worked in almost every series at Paramount, and Movies of the Week. I was in Mission Impossible, Mod Squad, My Friend Tony, my own television series "Nobody's Perfect" which lasted one season, and more than 300 episodic programs and forty-two motion pictures. I have Nat "King" Cole to thank for being a part of my film and television and music career.

Who would have thought a promotion gig with Nat "King" Cole would lead to television, commercials, and motion pictures? What vision can you put into action today? Set yourself in motion. Get that vision moving. Find out where you will end up!

**Fastrack**

Getting your "ticket punched" does not mean "kick back and relax." This would be the time to take Positivity to another level. No one ever achieved great things by reaching a level of comfort. Keep yourself pumped up and ready to go. Never forget what your job or your own company is expecting you to accomplish, then figure out a way to exceed their expectations and pave your own road to the top!

I remember getting on the plane and traveling to Los Angeles to meet the president of Liberty Records, Al Bennett. He was a real laid back kind of guy with an extremely high energy gear when it came to getting the job done.

The job was very simple. Get the records played, market them, sell them, then go to the next one and repeat the process. Do this with a wide range of music types like country, jazz, etc. This was a big leap from Nat "King" Cole and his label. This company, like Capitol, Sony, etc., put out thousands of records each year.

Meeting Al Bennett, owner, president, multi-millionaire was a trip because I never saw him wearing a suit in his office. As a matter of fact, after I joined the label around my sixth week, Al called me into his office. He asked me if I knew the dress code in California.

No suits. Shirts and pants, alpaca sweaters were acceptable. It was casual, casual, casual. This was the land where guys wore designer jeans, open collared shirts, sneakers or loafers, no socks and drove Ferraris, Mercedes, Lamborghinis, etc.

It was a far cry from New York. The main office for Liberty Records was huge. It housed more than 400 employees in the main building and another 400 or more at thirty-five different cities in the U.S. which made up their distribution centers.

The dress code gave the appearance of everyone taking the day off until you paid attention carefully and discovered the tremendous amount of work taking place. Liberty Records and Paramount studios became my home in more ways than one. I arrived to work before 6:00am and left long after 6:00pm. I did this because one or two (sometimes three or four) days, I was on a set at Paramount studios working on a different program.

I was truly in Hollywood. In my first year at Liberty, I bought a Jaguar XKE convertible brand new for $3,700. (that car now sells for $54,000 if you can find one). I was fortunate in my early days at Liberty because I had the opportunity to work with artists from Ravi Shankar to Jan & Dean and everything in between including Pop, Rock, Jazz, Easy Listening, R&B and Blues – even though I was head of the Black Music Department.

I met Jerry Lewis while promoting his son Gary Lewis & The Playboys fame. I almost got run over by a limousine trying to keep up with Jan & Dean at an autograph party and much more.

But the thing that is most important is that in a year's time, I was able to find employment for over 100 African-Americans in the distribution department. These men were my "men on the street" team for Jazz and R&B music. They more than paid for themselves by increasing sales by more than $15 million dollars in their first year.

I remember Al coming into my office. He asked me how we managed to get over 100 coloreds working for this company. Now Al was unique in that he owned half of Arkansas, and was truly from the south, but not a racist.

He congratulated me for seeing a need and finding a way to make it happen. He appreciated how I made sure that the expenses created a profit far above the cost of staff employed. They also generated a new market for this company. In addition he bumped me up to Senior V.P. status. That was a first for any African-American in a major corporation in music.

Everything was moving so fast now. My life seemed to become a blur, the prestige, the money, the opportunities were all great but I was wearing myself down rapidly.

A normal day started at five to six in the morning and didn't end till ten or eleven at night. Sometimes the wee hours of the morning. Talk about fast asleep, I was learning quickly how to sleep fast. Don't get me wrong, I was making the most money I ever had in my life. More than my parents ever thought to make, but I really needed to get a rest.

Early in my acting days/music promotion, I found something very special. I was beginning to affirm my vision, to do things before any other man of color had achieved. In the first two years, I was the first black actor to have a regular or recurring regular contract with the Gomer Pyle show and appeared in about thirty episodes.

I created and wrote the Afro Sheen Commercials ("black pride") commercials. I acted and also did the voice-overs. They appeared on "Soul Train." The most popular of these commercials was the one where I played the role of Frederick Douglas.

I had a recurring role on "Hill Street Blues" and was flying from St Croix in the U.S Virgin Islands to Los Angeles to film them. I had just built the first African-American-owned full production facility in the U.S. or the Virgin Islands.

Our first network production was the award winning "America's Paradise Triathlon" on NBC and syndicated to more than eighty-six countries. Our first triathlon was Lance Armstrong's first time (then sixteen-years-old) in a televised athletic competition. In this studio we also produced my original television series, "Through the Eyes of a Child."

See, positivity breeds more positivity! When you get a break, don't break it, make it stronger. Life was meant to be lived, not distracted. Keep moving forward positively and set your pace for success!

## Busy, Busy, Busy, Chaotic
## (and smiling)

I know at this point, you've read about some of the following stories. The important thing to gather here is, positivity becomes essential when you're dealing with reality. The busier you get, the more opportunity to fall into negativity or complacency. One of the best ways to lead an energetic and vibrant life is to purposefully incorporate positivity each and every day into your soul.

My acting career was going great, commercials, television episodes, motion pictures, and even two modeling jobs. I have the deepest respect for models. How the hell do they stand on their feet for hours at a time without moving?

Then with a simple command they move around like beautiful flowing streams filled with joy. Me? My first two modeling jobs were enough for me to know I definitely did not want to do that for a living.

At the end of a day, my legs, shoulders and feet felt like I had been beaten by someone with a soft whip. I could feel the pain slowly creep through my entire body.

 I love doing commercials though. I have been in commercials that featured national and international airlines, automobiles, dish soap, paper towels, McDonald's, wine, beer, car rentals, hair care products, in all, more than 70 commercials.

On stage, I played the lead in "One Flew Over the Cuckoo's Nest" on stage, for over a year. I never had so much joy being crazy for a few hours each night before an audience that enjoyed the entire production.

In the middle of all this, I was working on my next movie, television program, motivational presentations to young students and executives, and young athletes. I was flying high and enjoying all of the above.

Funny story was the night when Kelly (my son) and I were getting back from a long day of interviews and both of us were tired. Every time I asked my son what he wanted to eat his response was "room service Dad, room service." He liked the idea that someone would deliver to him all the junk food he could eat without having to do anything but wait for the delivery.

This was an incredible trip. We were heading to the west coast to finish up and go home. Oakland was the best and worst trip of my life. It was great for the movie, met with some old friends, had some great screenings, went to an Oakland Raiders game met a Cheerleader who later became my wife and the mother of my youngest two children. This was also the worst nightmare relationship of my life.

The cheerleader, a year later, would move in with me and my son and provide me with two incredible children whose lives I feel she single handedly destroyed via negative remarks and actions.

What a nightmare. Donna Summer became the God Mother of my two boys and daughter and my ex-wife did not want that to happen. She found ways to sabotage the lives of two great individuals, my youngest son and daughter. Before either of my youngest turned seven-years-old, we were divorced.

But life goes on and things happen. After my divorce I moved to the Virgin Islands. The Island of St. John first, then St. Thomas and finally St. Croix where I built (with my partners) the first African-American owned full production facility in the U.S. or Caribbean.

Our first project was "The Americas Paradise Triathlon" an incredible race that was second only to the "Ironman

Triathlon" in Hawaii. Americas Paradise was only the second major triathlon to make it to network television.

Our studio was covered by BET and verified us as the first full African-American owned production facility of its type in the U.S. or Caribbean. The fact that we were producing in its entirety the first program(s) for major network television like ABC, CBS, NBC, Golf Channel, and ESPN was incredible. It is a piece of history that will not be forgotten because we plan to become the "friendly reminder" very soon.

Some of the programming included a ninety-six city three-on-three basketball series called "Coup De Hoop" on ABC with the finale in Venice Beach California. Another was the JAG BMX World Championship Series on ESPN (now an Olympic Sport). Teens on the Green World Championship Series with youngsters from more than seventy countries competing, was produced for The Golf Channel. Coup de Hoop 2, CBS Sports, Americas Paradise Triathlon (NBC), were produced by Renny Roker Productions.

You can live many lives at the same time as long as they are all positive. Negativity will drag you down. A positive attitude is the only way to go.

# Stax Records and ROHAM

In the 1970's, the Watts riots in Los Angeles had everyone on edge. Stax Records became the official record company for the WattStax celebration to end violence in the Watts community. What better show of positivity than music?

Positive outlooks and actions tend to garner long-lasting results. Keep your mind and heart pointed in the direction of uplifting action and you will find more richness in your life than you could ever imagine.

On returning to Los Angeles after Hurricane Hugo, my partner, Forest Hamilton, and I formed ROHAM (Roker/Hamilton). We represented the famous Stax Records in California. We also stretched activities across the U.S. for music promotion.

We were a key force with WattStax's first sold out concert in L.A. Coliseum, (over 103,000 in attendance), the campaign for Isaac Hayes' Academy Award, and the sale of 500,000 gold albums with Johnny Taylor (first artist to have a single or album "go gold" solely in Southern California based on sales).

After Stax Records, I went back to acting and was in three movies and about thirty episodic television series. I had signed to co-star in four motion pictures which were all due to film close to back-to-back, which would solidify my acting career. As luck would have it, after co-starring in John Schlessinger's "Honky Tonk Freeway," I was ready for the next film when the longest strike in motion picture history began.

I was a single parent with my son Kelly, and we had just moved into our first house and were enjoying it. With all contracts cancelled, I was beginning to panic. I went to see my old friend Cecil Holmes at Casablanca Records, who asked me to join the company.

It wasn't long until Parliament/Funkadelic, Cameo, Village People, KISS, Donna Summer and others exploded and became super-stars and Casablanca Records was considered the hottest record company in the industry.

Donna Summer became my kids' Godmother. I ended up owning the P-Funk Tour with my partner Barry Fey in Colorado. Together we achieved top-five-grossing major-facilities promoters of buildings that held 60,000 people and greater for six consecutive years

Positivity not only impacts your life, it spreads to others. When your purpose is to always move in positive directions, the impact on our world becomes immeasurable. Positivity is not a part-time endeavor. Positivity is a life-long practice.

By stepping up at Stax and making history, we used positivity to improve our world. If more people would adopt this attitude, we could begin to rid our lives of all the oppressive negativity that threatens to engulf us. Stax grew out of an extreme environment, and positivity paved the way!

## Johnny Taylor Gold in California

When you set your mind to do something really big, I mean REALLY BIG, positivity is your best ally. Taking what you know, adding it to what you want, and fueling this with a positive outlook, the end results can dazzle!

Sometimes it's great to have a partner with the same or similar vision. When it works, it doubles the opportunity to succeed. That is what happened with my partnership with Roker-Hamilton, commonly known as ROHAM.

We were determined to demonstrate the importance of the African-American and Hispanic markets in the southern California market of the recording industry. While others had written off this market as unprofitable, we had a vision.

I recall a meeting with Al Bell, president of Stax Records. We were formulating a strategy that would enable Columbia Records (Sony Music) to tap into the African-American and Spanish markets in California. It was an effort to help the struggling Stax Records. Their profits had dropped significantly since joining Columbia Records.

We determined that the minority communities had no relationship with Columbia Distributors. But with singers like Isaac Hayes, Johnny Taylor, Staple Singers, Rufus Thomas and many more, there was reason to make that connection. Realizing that this was a unique market that required knowledge of the communities; we established a Sales/Marketing/Promotion staff with a focus on this market.

We created a program, establishing "foot soldiers" for the company. I called it the Retail Relations Group. Their purpose was to ensure that the retail coverage matched the "Air Play" in that market. We were confident that this would enable us to reach a market of millions of people. The sole purpose was to inform retailers, connecting them with Columbia's distributors and sales personnel.

Instead of hiring industry "experts", we put together a team of twelve black and Hispanic men and women. These individuals had little or no previous involvement in music business. They were young, energetic and visionary.

We used this opportunity to train our team on dealing with retailers and generating excitement for our recording artists. We taught them to build enthusiasm so that retailers would demand our records. This was an opportunity for many to "break into" the entertainment industry, a fast growing and lucrative business.

Our campaign started with a "call in"; we called a store and offered them twenty-five free copies of a record if we heard it in the background. We would call the same store at least twice. The campaign was so popular that stores would call us with our records being played in the background. We were off to a good start.

We were making a difference in the small market with the 'mom and pop' music retailers. We were making an even bigger impact on the wholesale houses. This was significant since this was where many of the stores purchased their records.

Our team was popularizing our music in their communities. We created partnerships with our music store owners. We were part of the community. We helped store owners repaint their stores and set up displays. We were making a difference in the community. It was a financial gain for the community and the industry. It was being noticed.

Al Bell called me up one day right after he had received a sales report from Columbia brass. It was reported that sales in southern California had increased significantly and that the team he hired (ROHAM) was doing an incredible job. Mr. Bell put us to the challenge. He was going to introduce a new Johnny Taylor album in southern California first. This would be the ultimate test.

We pulled out all stops. First we contacted the local radio stations and alerted them to west coast exclusivity. They could announce that only their region was hearing this new album. Then we told every local retailer that the local radio stations were going crazy playing it. We built excitement.

Our vision was to reign supreme in this highly competitive market. We gave out free albums to retailers if they played it in the store exclusively during certain hours. Within three weeks, southern California retailers sold over 500,000 copies. We made history. No artist in the history of music business ever went gold with sales exclusively in just southern California. This was great news! Our vision was now a reality!

Realities on this level do not usually happen with a negative, stressed, and angry demeanor. Yes, the work can be tough, but when you step into what you're doing with love in your heart for the task, you see what you can accomplish?

# Isaac Hayes' Academy Award

Doing something that no one has ever done before has a way of producing tremendous pride in one self. To dare to become the first to do anything is extremely thrilling, but to accomplish the feat takes guts and blind faith.

The first time in the history of the motion picture industry that a man of color won an Academy Award for an original score for a motion picture was Isaac Hayes', "Theme from Shaft." Everyone said we were crazy by attempting to get Isaac Hayes the Academy Award. Positivity was very, very high and we were not going to give up.

Now it was time to really show that if you can envision it you should be able to do it! When my partner and I got together to determine how we could do even better, we often thought we might just be dreaming. But we set our sights high. We realized that none, if any of the judges would listen to the soundtrack or watch the movie.

Cable television was just getting started. Many companies were using it to show movies for consideration in the Academy Awards. We decided "why not?" We booked Shaft in every time slot that we could. We then sent the soundtrack to as many voters as we could. We bought billboards promoting the music and asking for votes.

We worked closely with top public relations firms to plan stories about Isaac's charitable donations worldwide. We blasted his photo and story in every publication that we could. Our intentions were to make sure everyone that votes hears Shaft and sees Isaac's face daily.

We had a vision and we made it work. Isaac Hayes won his first and only Academy Award in 1972. He became the first Academy Award winner of color for an original soundtrack.

It was a great lesson even for us who created the plan. Once you create a vision, execution is critical, even when people tell you it can't be done. Stay focused on your outcome and stay focused on execution. You can make it happen if you believe and stay with it.

## Donna Summer and ExLax

She was beautiful. She was talented. She didn't give up.
Neither did we. Our plan worked for both of us. What you can
do with a positive attitude sometimes works in not so
mysterious ways…

While I was at Casablanca Records, we seemed to be focused
on creating a new promotion every day. Keeping the energy,
enthusiasm and creativity going was sometimes challenging.

We had the good fortune to have great leadership and support.
Neil Bogart, owner and president of Casablanca, was a true
visionary. He encouraged our department to think and work
"outside the box."

We did, and sometimes we were successful beyond our own
imagination. This was particularly true for one of our
campaigns - Donna Summer.

Donna was a very special lady to me. While the rest of the
world thought that she was a sex symbol, I knew her well. She
was a polite, religious, family person. She was a real lady. In
fact, she was godmother to my children.

Donna had created a fifteen minute song. There was no way we
could promote a song to radio stations that played no songs
longer than three minutes. We had thirty days to make this
happen, otherwise Casablanca Records was going to lose her as
a client. This was too big of an opportunity to lose.

I called a special conference with my regional promotion men. We had to take quick action that would be successful right from the start. We all threw in ideas.

Gary Byrd from Cleveland shared that there was an all-night DJ that loved Donna's new song, "Love to Love You Baby." The DJ was trying to get his manager to play the song, but wasn't having much success.

He hadn't given up. Gary had his mother bake brownies. He was going to return to the station later that night to deliver them. As Gary was telling the story, Bob yelled out "Exlax!"

There was a lot of snickering and laughing on the line. "Exlax in the brownies. There's nobody at the station with the all night guy. Give him the brownies. Put Exlax in them. If you put in enough, he's going to need time in the bathroom. He will welcome a fifteen minute song."

About an entire bottle of Exlax went into those brownies. Gary drove them over to the radio station, arriving just before the all night show began. The Donna Summer album was on top of the console. Gary was confident that the DJ was going to play it.

The unfortunate fact was, however, the General Manager asked the DJ to return it. Gary simply set the album and the brownies down. He hadn't been there two minutes before the DJ was already on the third brownie.

It didn't take long before the DJ became terribly uncomfortable. He suddenly jumped up and asked Gary to play Donna Summer's "Love to Love You Baby", the fifteen minute version.

Within five minutes, all of the phone lines were lit up. Gary heard calls from the bathroom to pick up the phones. He did. They were listeners calling to say that they loved the song.

By the time the song was just about finished, there was a shout from the bathroom, "Play it again. I'm stuck in here!"

The phones all lit up again. People were real excited now. Midway through the song the DJ emerged, walking slowly so as not to disturb anything. He began answering calls. Everyone loved Donna's song.

Then the phone with the big red light rang. It was the station owner. He was ecstatic.

"Fantastic! I have friends, clients, and even those that are not friends calling me regarding this incredible song. Keep it on as long as the calls keep coming in. Congratulations, you really know your stuff. You get a raise for this one!"

The rest is history. It was a vision that really worked! Her career took off after that record broke. Our dedication to positively impact our world with a superstar-singer-in-waiting paid off in ways we did not see at the time. What a wonderful lady. What a great outcome.

## JAG BMX World Championship

Positivity, as I've stated before, fuels dreams. Yes, you must employ action to get things done. Yes, you must have a plan for what you're doing. Most of all, you need a positive outlook to make the best possible outcome a reality. Sometimes, the reality is so sweet…

Ernie Alexander of the National BMX Association and myself were discussing the lack of multi-cultural participation at major events in the U.S.  Ernie reached into his draw and produced hundreds of letters from BMX'ers from around the world. He was going to throw them away. When asked to give them to me he asked, why?  "So we can produce the greatest and largest BMX event in history," I replied.

Ernie and I had a dream that youngsters from around the world could meet and compete and enjoy the best Christmas of their life. Not only did they enjoy it, not only did they like it; they demanded we do it again. And we did.

The time and effort to accomplish this event was incredible, but the results were unbelievably fantastic. Imagine seeing more than 3,000 bikes turned upside down with their owners ranging from five to sixty-five-year-old male and females. Most of them raced in two categories and sometimes three. More than 6,000 races per day were unheard of at that time. This called for an incredible "can do" effort.

I watched Ernie and his crew, made up of BMX track officials from around the world, all volunteer to ensure our success. It was magic. Team and race directors from around the world all volunteered to be a part of the greatest and largest event in BMX history to that point.

How could this happen to me? I was already too busy. I was deeply involved with BMX, I was promoting records for Casablanca Records, I was appearing in television programs, commercials and movies. I was raising a family and trying to make time for those things that I loved; tennis and golf. I found myself with a BMX bike company and team.

This was my new life - registering kids from around the world while promoting the events. I remember trying to sell ABC Sports on televising our JAG BMX World Championship. I was at the office of a BMX track owner that housed the governing body of the National Bicycle Association (NBA).

I was meeting with Ernie. I remember that he was having a difficult time opening his desk drawers. They were filled with those letters from around the world asking questions about his track and BMX.

Once I had the letters in hand, I had a vision. I was going to invite all of those that sent Ernie a letter, an invitation to the World Championship of Bicycle Moto-Cross. I had a vision that we were promoting and producing the largest and greatest BMX event ever held in the world.

Ernie looked at me like I was crazy at first, while I was stuffing all the post cards and letters into a shopping bag that I found in his office. As I stuffed, I shared my vision with Ernie. I suggested Chicago or Indianapolis. He continued to look at me as if I was crazy. His look was especially baffled when I suggested that we hold it during the Christmas season.

I asked Ernie one simple question. "What time of the year does almost every student in the world have a vacation?"

"Christmas!" said Ernie.

I responded, "Best time of the year! When do parents wish there was something their children could afford or really want to do during long holidays?"

We were both parents of active children so it didn't take long to determine what we were doing this holiday season. "Looks like I'll be running the JAG BMX World Championship!" And he did.

There were a plethora of BMX bicycle companies around the world. There were six sanctioning bodies in the United States, plus one for every country. We had our work cut out for us. We had to get the word out to the world.

We extended an invitation to all of the sanctioning bodies and offered to pay them two dollars per entry from their members, give them a free room at a hotel, plus provide free entry for their own kids (up to four youngsters).

This was now a recognized event. Coca-Cola agreed to be our name-in-title sponsor. Hence it was called "THE COCA-COLA JAG BMX World Championship"! We made sure that every country that might consider participating knew that we had a sponsor. We had mock trophies made up and sent photos of our ten-foot first place trophy around the world. It was very impressive. Mail began pouring in. Tickets were being sold.

We kept our sponsors and the sanctioning bodies updated on our progress. Even they were impressed. At one point, we had more participants coming from outside the United States than within.

We were promoting television exposure. We knew that if we had to we could film it and we could broadcast it elsewhere. When ABC Sports (ESPN) came onboard, the event really got hot. We had close to 1,000 riders by late October. These were the days before e-mail and on-line registration. We asked countries to register at the venue or our official hotel when they arrived.

With still over two months to go, I sat back and actually saw a vision of thousands of bikes turned upside down with youngsters all working on their bikes. My vision was coming true. This was going to be The World Championship of BMX! The event was going to look like a World Championship too! Early projections suggested that we would have 1,000 - 2,000 riders. Both Ernie and I knew the numbers would be much larger.

Ernie had ordered our wooden jumps and starting gate. They were just about completed with only a small amount of painting still to be completed. The massive starting gate had Coca-Cola on it when it was opened and closed. It was also on the descent of the starting hill, plus in forty other locations all around and near the track.

On the evening the last entrant signed up, we had over 4,000 entrants. More than eighteen hotels were filled and that didn't count local riders and friends of local riders staying at their homes or those staying in hotels outside of the downtown area.

Mayor William Hudnut sent us an invitation to meet him at his office. He asked me to bring a few of the kids participating in the race with me. I brought children from Australia, Europe, Asia, South America and United States. There were at least fifty countries represented. We were ushered into the Mayor's office where we were presented with the keys to the city.

For the five years that we produced the BMX World Championship, more than 40,000 room nights were booked each year. We had a vision that really exceeded our wildest imagination. It all started with one vision:

1. Global event

2. International sponsors

3. First BMX event on television worldwide

4.  First BMX with International television broadcast

5.  First BMX event with major global sponsors

6.  First BMX event that involved and benefitted six U.S. governing bodies and more than forty International governing bodies or country team reps

7.  Key to the city of Indianapolis

Positivity, it fuels dreams. Yes, you must employ action to get things done. Yes, you must have a plan for what you're doing. Mostly, you need a positive outlook to make the best possible outcome a reality. Sometimes, the reality is so sweet…

# The Mothership Tour

When no one thinks you can successfully pull something big off, positivity better be in your toolkit. This one took the police chief, the mayor, and a huge herd of high schoolers who promised to be good (and was) to pull this off.

The Mothership Tour debuted in Chicago and drew 89,000 persons in a facility that holds 79,000. No arrests, no problems, just a bunch of tired people after the show because the music never stopped.

This was the way we began and continued to sell out every major outdoor facility we occupied. Our vision was very simple, give the audience non-stop, positive, and upbeat music till they were too tired and could only snap their fingers.

The really exciting event was the Mothership Tour Stop in Los Angeles that sold over 103,000 tickets. The event almost didn't happen. It was in the middle of a gasoline strike otherwise known as "No Gas at the Pumps" in Los Angeles.

I really had a strong vision on this one. There was only one person in the city of Los Angeles, Mayor Bradley, who I needed to pull this off. But first I had to make a trip to the Chief of Police and the Transportation Deptartment.

Ok, that was done. Now it was time to make an appointment. I was surprised the Mayor remembered me. What a great man. I told him that I was producing a concert in the Los Angeles Coliseum primarily for young persons. I mentioned it was called the Mothership Tour.

The mayor looked at me quizzically and asked "You don't expect me to attend do you?"

"No sir," was my reply. "I do expect about 100,000 youngsters to attend."

Mayor said "That sounds like trouble, including lots of arrests."

"No sir. I met with the Chief of Police and he loves my idea. He says that it could be one of the best self-discipline major events to ever take place."

The mayor was interested. With the gas shortage going on, youngsters that did drive couldn't afford to go.

The Mayor continued, "And what if it doesn't go the way you say it will."

"I would go to jail for lying."

The Mayor looked at me and said, "You really believe you can do this? You really feel this can happen? Do you realize what this could mean to this city? This would be incredible positive publicity Renny", the Mayor said. "So in as few words or better tell me why these youngsters would not misbehave?"

"Very simple," I said. "They will not be allowed back on the bus to go home. They can't call someone to come and get them, there is almost no gas in the city except your supply," I said.

The Mayor then added, "Did you really meet with the Chief of Police?"

"Yes Sir. I did and he should be here in five minutes."

No sooner did I say it than he showed up and confirmed his support.

The idea worked. More than 103,000 showed up. We had one arrest. We all celebrated one of the largest concerts in the history of Los Angeles, and definitely the least arrests, and no fights. No one was hurt or injured. Tired and perspiring, Yes! Trouble? No way!

I was positive the Mayor would be happy. I was called to his office that next Monday. The Mayor looked me dead in the eye and said, "You had one arrest."

"Yes sir," was my response as I stood at his desk in disbelief.

Then he said very excitedly, "That's incredible!" He reached out and shook my hand.  I think I skipped all the way home. That was incredible. That was fantastic. That was one hell of a payday for me. I was excited, positive and certain I could do it again and did! Heck, I was positive we could do it the first time!

## From Poop to President

When all is said and done, a positive view on what we do lifts not only ourselves, but those around us, to new levels. This attitude shift is not something you can do part-time. No, to achieve dreams and goals in this world, a full-time positive view, no matter our position, can lead us to better places.

When thinking of yourself and who you are, the impressions of others do not truly define your worth. You do. Positive attitudes toward yourself and who you are and what you do often become our greatest strengths, as long as you will allow them. Conversely, a low opinion of ourselves brings with it less than stellar results.

I hosted a motivational class for the California Board of Tourism. My first class was attended by a janitor, a receptionist, sales people, and a few presidents of major hotel groups.

Each person in the group introduced himself/herself to the others. They shared a brief description of his/her job. Everyone seemed proud of their positions. I asked all of them, including the presidents, if they intended to rise up the ladder of their jobs. Responses were great and everyone was positive about the future, until we reached Jessie.

Jessie was the custodian at his office building and seldom saw any of the other employees. He had a way of making sure every bathroom in the building was sparking clean. Every glass door and window were perfectly clear. He made sure absolutely no mess was left on the floors.

When someone spilled something on his highly polished hallways or office floors, he quietly cleaned it up. Nothing got past Jessie. Many staff members bragged about their spotless bathrooms and clean environment, but they never knew who was responsible for doing all this work. Many thought there had to be a crew of at least four or five people.

When it came to Jessie's turn to speak, he started to leave the room. I stopped him by calling out his name and asking him to come back to his seat please. Jessie stopped, walked back to his chair, and looked at me hard. He said his name followed by, "I'm just the janitor and I'm not sure why I am here. This must be a mistake."

I looked him straight in the eye and told him "This is not a mistake. You are one of the most important persons in this room."

The looks I got could choke a snake. A few presidents and most of the audience looked at me as though I were crazy.

I began by telling this young man that when your bathrooms are sparkling and clean, then every visitor feels comfortable being in the building and working with the respective staff members. But if it were nasty, toilet paper and paper towels on the floor, dirty or unflushed toilets, it reflects bad on the company.

About two weeks later the president of the company walked into one of the bathrooms rather than go back upstairs to his private bathroom. When he entered, he found the cleanest public bathroom he had ever seen. Upon leaving the bathroom he spotted Jessie and congratulated him on doing such a fine job.

Jessie called me after the encounter with the president and he told me that he tried for an executive position after college and was turned down. He also told me that he had placed six messages on the president's desk with suggestions for major changes potentially saving the company millions of dollars while earning significant dollars.

He continued to tell me that every suggestion was applied. The company was thriving because of these suggestions. Jessie never left his name on any of the suggestions. The president often wondered who this unknown person that had saved the company millions of dollars, while providing ways to increase their bottom line by millions of dollars.

I told Jessie to go home and call the president. Let him know that he was the person that left the notes, and give him enough of the content and dates you left them so he will believe you. He will see you. Wear a suit and tie and ask for a decent salary.

Jessie called the president's office and explained to his secretary that he was the one that left the president notes on his desk. The president asked Jessie to come to his office right away. When Jessie arrived he first was quizzed by the president to make sure he was the right person.

The president offered Jessie a job and an office right next to his. He also offered Jessie a salary of $250,000 per year. Jessie almost choked to death.  He only made minimum wage cleaning the bathrooms and halls etc.

The president took Jessie's choking as disapproval, so he raised it to $350,000. Jessie accepted the offer, shook hands and promised to be in the office early in order to provide additional suggestions for review.

Jessie looked at him with pride and said "I'm going to be your number one marketing person of this company. The president told him that he already is number one in his book. Jessie said I also have a recommendation for a new janitor. The president looked at him and wondered how Jessie knew the janitor had resigned?

 "As of today you are a marketing exec in progress. Welcome to our floor" It wasn't long until Jessie made Senior V.P. and six years later, president. Jessie went from Poop to President.

Positivity requires a belief in oneself. If you are not willing to step up to your true potential, how can you expect to succeed? This is one of the major hurdles everyone must master. Will you step into your positivity and your success? Or will you continue to muddle in mediocrity? I say, "Choose Positivity!"

# Self Esteem

Self esteem is very important if you want to become successful. To know you can deliver is a powerful feeling, and to let others know you can do it is a powerful statement. Self confidence and positive delivery are incredible tools to have in your corner. Show them you can deliver with a confident smile.

There were many times I knew we could deliver and usually everything rode on the first event. I knew it would establish the baseline for our long term relationships with our top clients. This was very important for success with the companies mentioned in this book.

Some people call it bragging, some call it egocentric, and others just plain "braggadocios." But there is another term not utilized enough in the competitive field and that is self-esteem. It's like the man or woman who just lost fifty pounds and walks by a mirror, stops and steps back into the mirror image and declares the image awesome.

If you could put it on camera you would call it pride, feeling good about yourself, even a second and third look is ok. Too often, many people won't acknowledge their own beauty, handsomeness, and most of all, the ability to get the job done or the problem fixed.

Have you ever watched a person walk into a room, smile, and impress everyone in the room with their demeanor?  Self-esteem and egomania are two different things, just like feeling good about yourself versus telling everyone how great you are.

Most people enjoy others who feel good about themselves and their particular choice of endeavor. Walk into a room with a sense of pride, an "I'm-willing-to-do-whatever-it-takes-to-make-it-happen" mood and demeanor, versus I will crush anyone in my way to get it done!

 The way to possess confidence in yourself is to accomplish the feat or task set before you, or gain the knowledge through careful study, analysis. Actually, there is a definite sense of pride that is overwhelming when you believe deep in your heart, mind and soul "I can do this!"

Leaders of organizations, corporations and institutions are aware and on the alert for individuals who have a combination of dignity, ability, creativity, wholesomeness, and desire to achieve by using the resources available to them, beginning with supportive staff.

Self-esteem sends a message to everyone we encounter, as does our pride in our work. Our self-confidence comes from "having done it before," having recognized the challenge, problem or obstacles in our way and having the ability to step up to the challenge. We remove the problem and remove all obstacles in our way providing an opportunity for success.

A perfect example of this is the Thom McAnn Jox Jag BMX Shoe which was made possible by a $75 sponsorship (originally $50,000). It actually turned into a multi-million dollar opportunity for our company. At no point did we ever feel we would fail, nor did any of our staff. That's when pride, dignity, teamwork, creativity, a sense of humility, mixed with a "can-do attitude" reverberates among those in power in major corporations.

Take a moment to assess yourself and the potential project or company you will be associated with. Ask yourself, "Am I ready for this? Am I confident? Are my self-esteem and confidence in the proper position for success?" Stand up straight, get your act together, and succeed.

## It Takes a Vision and a Great Team

To have a vision and be willing to make it happen is one of the greatest feelings in the world. It takes careful creation, planning, funding, and implementing. In order to do that, it takes careful planning and the right people as part of your team. Your vision can become a reality if you want it to.

Stay positive. Stay true to your vision. Develop the energy and stamina to see it through. You will go places you never dreamed possible…

If you had to "sell" a vision, which do you suppose would be easier to hock, one that is positive, or one that is negative. Of course, everyone knows the answer to that question. So why don't we take the path of positivity more often? The list that follows would never have happened without a positive, can-do attitude!

Since my first sports television series in 1979, I've had one vision. But before I tell you about this vision, there are a few people who made the beginning happen for me in sports. Bob Eiger, CEO at Disney and an incredible visionary, and Roone Arledge (RIP) one of, if not the greatest, name in sports production. Roone was the former President of ABC Sports and creator of The ABC Wide World of Sports Series. He also was the first to use ten cameras on an Olympic 100 meter race and much more.

The two of them are responsible for me becoming the first African American to produce his own sports series, the Jag BMX World Championship Series. Boy did I have a lot to learn. Yes, I made mistakes. We also pulled off a few brilliant moves.

Actually seeing our program on television (which debuted on ESPN in the early days 1979-84 and was syndicated to over eighty countries, all military bases and all naval ships at sea), gave me an idea. Thank you Bob and Roone.

There was always a clear vision of the things that had to be done to accomplish our goal. I realized very quickly that envisioning is just the beginning.  Making it happen necessitates a great plan, facts, timeline, and the people who can support both financially and creatively.

You need to have a team of people willing to work hard because they believe in your plan. You also need the financial support, or a creative way to bypass up-front funding by creating a model of your plan which shows sponsors and or investors why they should support it before it happens is essential.

**Major team projects in my life included:**

Nat King Cole - Finding his last hit "Ramblin Rose" then convincing him to record it.

First black executive in music business at Liberty Records - Creating a team of seventy-five people who wanted to be more than warehouse staff and converted them to part-time marketing and promotion staff which produced more than fifteen million dollars in record sales via getting airplay and sales through retailers. The marketing and promotion of more than 200 recording artists who won a minimum of one gold and/or platinum album/CD per artist. Many had multiple albums/CD's which sold millions of copies

Isaac Hayes - The campaign to make him the first man of color to win an Academy Award for Original Music Soundtrack with "The Theme from Shaft."

Columbia Records (Sony Music) -- First person in history to lead a special sales and promotion team that sold 500,000 copies of an album (gold album) solely in Southern California.

Donna Summer staff - which was an "outside-the-box" creative venture which used Ex-Lax to get a radio on-air personality to play a fifteen minute version of "Love to Love You Baby" which unleashed a brilliant career.

The Jag BMX World Championship, the first televised global BMX event in history on ESPN and the first African American to produce his own sports event for network television.

The Americas Paradise Triathlon - first triathlon to begin on one island and end on another island. This event was produced for NBC television (first African American to produce a sports event for NBC Sports). The production was done by our Studio (also first African American full production facility ever built).

Coup de Hoop Three-on-Three Basketball Series took place in ninety-six cities at the same time and had its finale at Venice Beach, California.  Another first for ABC. In its second year, it was on CBS.

The ownership and promotion of The Mothership Tour - (featuring Parliament/Funkadelic for six consecutive years)

sold out each year a minimum of forty major venues each year including Los Angeles Coliseum: 103,000; Soldiers Field Chicago over 80,000 etc. Along with partner Barry Fey.

One year sold out three major facilities - without using radio, television, or print advertising but used a high school, in-school radio network (lunch time in cafeteria in multiple schools) in each city.

Co -produced and starred in Johnny Tough - a "G" rated family movie that was the first African American film to reach number one in Daily Variety box office sales

All my acting life I wanted to play the role of a mentally deranged individual on stage; and that was first African American approved by the author to play the lead on stage (Los Angeles, CA.) of "One Flew Over the Cuckoo's Nest."

Creation of the first minority-owned junior golf program which is truly international - "Teens on the Green" helped more than 2,000 youngsters earn scholarships to college. Also, it was the first junior golf program to be aired on The Golf Channel. This program went to more than thirty-five countries, built satellite operations in more than seventy-five countries and was televised in each country.

In each of the above, there was a vision that not only set the stage for everything, but an action plan to accomplish them. It was not a wake-up-in-the-morning-and-just-do-it. "It" was carefully and strategically planned based on a vision that said, "Just do it!" Make sure your vision is properly and carefully thought out and that you are ready to implement the "plan" for your vision. Then roll up your sleeves and get to work.

In almost all of the above we were told "It is impossible to do!"

To have a vision and be willing to make it happen is one of the greatest feelings in the world. It takes careful creation, planning, funding, and implementing. Stay positive. Stay true to your vision. Develop the energy and stamina to allow positivity to see it through. You will go places you never dreamed possible…

## Dreams Do Come True

Do whatever you feel you can do - but be smart about it. Take chances, thought-out chances, which can change your life. Stay upbeat, don't fear work, and embrace what you love. Think about this – if you don't love your work, how can you possibly embrace it in positivity?

All of us dream almost every night and many times during the day with our eyes wide open. Too often we don't playback that dream or think about accomplishing it - especially if it is positive and good for you and your future. I had a dream. I chased it, lived it, and loved it. Enjoy your dream.

I had a vision of Otto Preminger endorsing me at Paramount Studios. I also had a vision that Liberty Records hire the first African American executive, promoting Jan & Dean, Vicki Carr, Jackie DeShannon, Chipmunks, O'Jays, Jimmy McCracklin, and Bobby Vee.

One of my goals was to work steady at Paramount and other studios while building a career and reputation in acting. I also wanted to make sure I earned at least double what I'd already earned before  deciding to leave the record company.

I got the job at Liberty Records. It was a great place to work. For the first few weeks at the company I wore a suit or sport jacket, shirt and tie until the owner Al Bennet told me to relax and get into California-wear. This eliminated the need for shirts and ties, suits and sport jackets.

In the third month of employment, I found myself at a Liberty Records Convention in Chicago. Liberty had 3,300 employees and only three of them were persons of color: Irma Newton who was in charge of all album covers (big job) and Henry who cleaned the building and me - the first vice president of color at Liberty Records.

It turned out that Henry was not really the cleaning man he appeared to be. He was a millionaire partner of Al Bennett. Henry cleaned (with staff), Al's building and his staff cleaned the other 200-plus buildings they had under contract. My job was to make the company respected in the Black Music Division and sell records.

Liberty owned its own distribution in the United States and was one of the top three record companies in the world in sales. By adding the Afro-American R & B department, we could get to number two or even number one if we were successful.

We were indeed successful with little-known artists including the O'Jays and Irma Thomas, who all seemed to catch fire. These artists burned up the charts and garnered a great deal of air play on the radio.

Back to the vision. After visiting almost all of the distributers, it was apparent that it was wrong to depend on any of the staff of the distributers to promote the music in this division.

One distributer had recently hired an African American, Freddie, to work in the warehouse. Now Freddie was a very aggressive young man. He was taking records over to the radio station because he realized that the local promo guy did not want to go to those stations.

We spoke for quite a while and I gave him all the info he needed to tell the local stations. The programming heads welcomed having a local rep from the distributor call on them.

The vision was very clear: get each distributor to hire a stock room/promotion person to hit all the rhythm and blues and jazz stations on certain days of the week and on all other days work in the warehouse.

Within two months we had over seventy persons of color working on our product and we were nine million dollars over projected income. These guys not only knew the radio stations, they knew all the retailers and wholesalers because they spoke with them daily regarding delivery of records, etc. The team was getting stronger: "Renny's Army" they were called by our company owned distributers.

One day Al called me into his office. He started the meeting by congratulating me on our tremendous increase in sales. Then he seemed to be trying to figure out how to say something. That wasn't like Al, he spoke what he felt quite easily.

He told me that we had hired over seventy-five "coloreds" since I started working there. My reply, "They are not coloreds. They are African Americans," I reminded him. "And they are great workers who bring in more money per person single handedly than anyone else in this division." Al smiled and told me he was well aware of that and gave me a raise.

While working for Liberty, I met Jerry Lewis through his son of "Gary Lewis & The Playboys," fame. As a matter of fact, I met a lot of "big name" stars, either through the artist on the label, or actors at Paramount Studios where I still worked almost every week. The vision was working, but fatigue was now a factor.

Because of my two jobs - acting and promotions - I would come to work early leave late.  Al Bennett called me in one day and asked me if I wanted to kill myself. He said that Henry, his cleaning company partner, told him I'm in every morning at 5:00am, and one of the other employees who work late shifts says I never leave before 9:00pm at night.

I went home that night with Mr. Nat "King" Cole's message ringing in my ear: "Do not leave your day job because you are in a few television shows or movies."

At that point I was working at least forty-six weeks a year at Paramount, earning twice what was earned at the record company - and without any hassles. But I kept my "day job" anyway, at least for the next seven years, before going after a bigger and better acting career. The vision was working overtime.

Do you see?  Do whatever you feel you can do - but be smart about it. Take chances, thought-out chances, which can change your life. Stay upbeat, don't fear work, embrace what you love. If you don't love your work, how can you possibly embrace it with positivity?

# People are Important

People are important! Do not take them for granted. People are important. Nurture your relationships. People are important. Stay in touch but don't be a pest, be an asset, a friend, a communicator of positive information!

One key aspect of positivity is interpersonal relationships with business people. Too often we miss opportunities because we look out for ourselves first. We don't invest the time to look around or to find willing and able help.

One of the greatest opportunities me and my team had prior to making a major deal with Coca-Cola was the opportunity to work with their local bottlers and key sales persons. What I did was build a grass roots promotion that constantly increased the Coca-Cola bottom line and the trust of the bottlers that we would always deliver.

It got to the point that when we discussed promotions, we would co-promote or we would promote with complete visibility of our procedures and activities. After a while, the relationship was so open to everyone involved that we were copied on inter-office opinions and suggestions.

At one of these disclosures, the bottler sent us a letter stating that they never figured we would be able to pull off what we had drawn up as a "definite results promotion" with 100% delivery promised to the bottler in attendees, product to be sold, and consensus from the community.

In this letter, the bottler clearly stated that he did not expect us to be successful in delivering what we promised. But we knew we could. We promised it, so we delivered it.

The bottler also discussed the fact that in the past we had sold out the L.A. Sports Arena more times than any other promotion in the facility. We had also sold out (at the time) the Coliseum (103,000 spectators) more than anyone. Despite those feats of accomplishments they never thought we could sell out 18,000 seats based on a BMX activity.

Not only did we sell out the facility, we did so multiple times, and the bottler was more than pleased. What we did was make sure that the leaders within the Coca-Cola organization were informed every time we were doing something in their area.

Whether they were sponsors or not, we made sure that Coca-Cola was invited to participate in a manner that was beneficial to the bottlers. In all cases, we made sure that the home office was aware (especially Mr. Dunn), of our progress.

He received copies of letters from the bottlers, especially the head of the Los Angeles Bottler (considered one of the biggest in the country). It got to the point where the bottler would call us when they had a special promotion to see if we wanted to participate with them!

We catered to all the people in power by delivering on our word and exceeding all predictions. At Thom McAnn Shoe stores, we ranked in the top three sneakers in almost every state. We created our own communications with their shoe store managers, informing them of local JAG BMX Riders in their city.

Many of our youngsters would place autographed photos in stores or hold a bike safety or local event autograph signing for neighborhood youngsters.

With Post Cereal, we began a free breakfast for riders and their families with Post Cereal products, capped off with a surprise that the whole family could enjoy. In all cases we provided video, photos and personal comments regarding our sponsors from parents, participants and spectators.

At all times we made sure that all Coca-Cola leaders from the President/CEO of each company to the local representatives of these and other companies were aware of our promotions.

Our creating and producing of events, television, and marketing promotions were an integral part of our footprint. It was important that we inform a wide range of people on all levels not only of our successes but on questions about the brands we represented. Sometimes we would receive suggestions about our sponsors and things we could do to increase our representation of each of our sponsors.

But our informing did not begin and end with our corporate sponsors. Depending on the project the Governor, Mayor and other political figures would receive positive information. Tourism, Chambers of Commerce and adult and youth organizations leaders would be made aware of our positive activities.

Several times we interfaced with local tourism agencies because of the incredible amount of room sales we could generate in conjunction with many of our events and projects.

Sharing information was important to our recipients and therefore important to all of us. Keeping everyone informed, we literally made sure that all recipients had a blow by blow breakdown of the event and a very short overview for those that did not have the time but could refer back to details if necessary.

Whenever I was in the town of one of our current or prospective sponsors, we would invite them to breakfast, lunch, dinner or just a brief update on projects that filled their needs in multiple areas. In the end, when it's all said and done, all positive projects and results were shared with those partially or completely interested in our activities, or those that might be interested later.

People are important! Do not take them for granted. People are important. Nurture your relationships. People are important. Stay in touch but don't be a pest. Be an asset, a friend, a communicator of positive information!

## Big Time Chicago Concert

When you achieve success, positivity is not something you may now throw aside. In fact, you will find that survival and enjoyment of your success will require larger doses of a positive attitude than you previously employed.

I'm always amused by the amount of enemies a person can collect by being aggressive, persuasive, talented, creative, positive, focused, energetic, and most of all very sincere.

Somehow, you feel like you are the only person in this position until you began to communicate with others like yourself. I also listened to people that felt they had the "lowdown" on people like me. I listened to some of the most ridiculous stories I ever heard in my life.

I remember one of the first major concerts of which I was a part owner. This concert would take place in Chicago at Soldiers Field. Funny thing was that right before the event another similar concert to mine had cancelled, and the police, the facility, and local residents were really concerned about a riot if my concert ended the same way.

The night before the event, more than 60,000 people brought fold up chairs, blankets, etc. to enjoy the rehearsal and verify that the artists were really in town. On that night, we sold out and my partner and I were celebrating. Sound-check was going great. Thousands outside were looking forward to being able to see their favorite artist. It was awesome.

We had met with a popular black college organization and asked them to assist us by providing college students to lead attendees to locations to witness this historic event. At that time, it was about to become the largest event of its type in Chicago's history. Although the arena held 79,000 people, we were at 79,300 sold tickets prior to show time and there were thousands still waiting for the box office to open in the morning.

Parliament/Funkadelic, Bootsy, Barkays, Confunksion, Taste of Honey, and more were expected to perform. Our host was Tom Joyner. We had promised the college one dollar per attendee as a donation. At that point, they would receive more than $79,000 in exchange for one-day assistance by students.

It doesn't get better than this. It made all of us proud to know that we would provide the college with a very large contribution. The next day, not one college student showed up. We really needed their assistance, but somehow the entire crowd knew the magnitude of this event. They saw it becoming an open door for more events to follow if this one was successful.

The crowd was incredible. The concert was incredible. The next day I went to the college with a certified check for $89,000. I remember the look on the college president's face when he saw the check. His mouth dropped and he looked like he was struck by lightning.

"I can't accept this check," he said. "We did not show up as promised." He explained to me how many times the college had agreed to assist concert promoters and never received a dime. He told me that he was concerned about the safety of his students with the size of this event.

Part of me understood what he was saying and yet a promise is a promise. I told him to pretend that the students did show up. I would endorse them as having done a great job. I would endorse them because they needed the money and was burned too often in the past by other promoters.

Before leaving his office I recommended that every promoter that promised assistance should put it in writing. He just shook his head in disbelief as he looked at his certified check. I smiled and exited his office. This indeed was incredible – actually, better than incredible.

Even though our company had to deal with the negativity brought on by promoters before us, we were able to maintain a positive attitude and do the right thing. Just because someone shows themselves initially as an enemy, or a non-supporter, that fact should not change your tenacity to stay positive.

## The Bronx Zoo

Good things come from mysterious beginnings. At times these beginnings may seem a bit rough around the edges. After all, nothing in our lives is perfect. Yet, if you can stop and take a look, a good, long positive look, most circumstances work out in the end if you can choose the positive path of sight. My father taught me this…

Growing up in the Bronx at the time, we did not have much money. We used to go to the Bronx zoo. One day my Dad told my Mom there was a way to get into the zoo for free, just walking across a field.

My mom protested, but my dad insisted. We went to find this secret location my dad found. He was right. This giant open field in front of us held a stairway leading up to the zoo walkway with lots of people enjoying the zoo. My father grabbed my hand and we began walking across what looked like baked dirt. The dirt appeared that it once was muddy and now was a dry field just waiting for the Roker family to cross.

We took about twelve strides and began sinking so fast it scared me. The sinking was so immediate, my fright was overwhelming. My father yelled out for help and sank another six inches, so I yelled and we both sank.

By this time hundreds gathered on the railing above watching us as we struggled. My mother was crying, my sister was crying, but it looked like nobody cared. They just looked at us. It seemed only moments later my dad was in up to his chest and me to my waist. Now I was crying too and really scared.

Just when I thought death was next, two guys with ladders shoved them out to us. We grabbed the rope attached to the ladders. I arrived first, then my dad to dry land. My mother was beside herself, my dad calm.

When we arrived at the zoo office, instead of being met by the police, we met the manager. He had clothes for me and my dad (better than what we were originally wearing). He also presented us with a hot shower, lifetime VIP pass for entire family, access to the high priced private train that ran through the park, and a very tasty lunch, that we really needed (I was always hungry).

When my mother said, "Reggie, see what you did?" my dad replied, "Yes I do. Free admittance, first class service, and oh yes, even free food when we go to the zoo."

The ability to see the good, even while you are closely wrapped in frightening circumstances, opens up many options you may never have seen or even planned. The sooner you can turn a negative, frightening situation to a positive in your life, the better your life will be.

POSITIVITY

## Sisters and Brothers, Love and Hate

Family and positivity do not always go hand in hand. It takes effort. Someone must make the effort. All it takes is one person. Embrace positivity in your familial relationships.

Amazing how your family has such a tremendous impact on your life. My older brother (only brother) is an example. I worshipped him as a teenager. His singing group had sold over a million records multiple times. As an adult he made the careers of many recording artists like Dion Warwick, Shirelles, Chuck Jackson and others.

At one time, he represented the top ten record companies for marketing and promotion for the entire country (I had the privilege to work with him). My brother was a genius and still is. What an impact on my life.

My oldest sister (eleven months younger) and I competed in everything imaginable, especially school grades, reading, and communicating. I really believe that the level of competition to this day has created a love-hate relationship between us. When I say hate, it's more like a disagreement as to how each other lives, eats, communicates, and pays attention to details.

Then there is my younger sister whom I love dearly. She was always concerned about me. One time when I was working for Nat "King" Cole, I was out on the road for six weeks promoting "Ramblin' Rose" and a few recording artists on Mr. Cole's record label.

I had caught a bad cold and when I called home to see how everyone was doing. My sister begged me, and then demanded, I come home because I was sick. She accused me of not taking care of myself and she was worried about me. As a matter of fact, she cried on the phone.

I will never forget that moment and I love her dearly, but make no mistake, I love all of them. No cookie cutter brothers and sisters. They are all unique, and very, very special.

So what does this all mean? Quite simply that family love is very important. It's not how many times you call, visit or have family outings and barbecues. It's where they are in your heart.

It's the ability to not talk for months, then pick up the phone and feel like you just rediscovered your most favorite person in the world. I have tons of nieces, nephews, and cousins. Hopefully, one day before I die, I will see them all.

Then there are my children. Only one really understands me and one kind of understands me, one is adopted and two don't talk to me (their loss, not mine). I've already lived my life, knowing my parents and loving them and their loving me, as I love all my children (even those that don't communicate).

Family is important. My advice is that we all learn to get along with our family and close friends. No matter what we think or feel about each other as sibling or parents, we should remember to love one another despite any faults.

I was the "First African American" to accomplish many great things, and that is my legacy. Unfortunately, that success came at the cost of losing some of my family and wives, and friends. I like being alone and I love being in love with one person, while embracing the world I live, work and play in.

I am very happy now, and in the best physical condition of my life, working out every day (almost), and being loved and appreciated by the lady of my life. I love my work (whatever

that happens to be at the time) and I love the family that seems
to come and go.

Funny, it doesn't matter how many show up at my funeral
(whenever it may be, many years from now). It's how many
show up at my next accomplishment, like this book!

My advice to all of them and all of you is very simple. Love
the one you're with. Love the ones that support you, and for
God's sake, love the ones whose family blood is the same as
yours.

As a kid, Jackie Robinson Jr. told me he was going to beat up
my sister. He knew we were very competitive, and seemed to
dislike each other at times. I told him that if he even touched
my sister I would "kick his ass!"

He couldn't understand that, but I hope you do. You only have
one family. Hold on to them. Communicate with them. Love
them no matter what your differences might be.

Love and positivity go together very well. When you practice
one, you often practice the other. When it comes to family and
friends, your positive effort is the most important aspect you
add to the relationship.

## If You Can Dream It, You Can Do It

Dreams are simply opportunities waiting to happen. I was once told to "wish in one hand and spit in the other, and see which one fills up first." Ah, but what is missed there is that the wish you throw into your hands can become reality as long as you put those hands to use. Action brings dreams into reality. Positivity fuels action.

Is it real, or is it just in your mind? How many times can you remember dreaming or thinking about something so hard that you actually believe that you already accomplished it? Has that ever happened to you?

If so, you are not alone. You are right where you need to be. Now come out of the dream and make it a reality. An old saying is, "If you can dream it, you can do it." Now, are you really ready to challenge yourself and the world?

It's amazing sometimes how your mind can make you believe that you are truly accomplishing something when in fact it's just your mind going through the motions. Funny how that happens. It's like a dream of being in the boxing ring with a top boxer or wrestler or karate champ and beating the living daylights out of them.

You move and escape a thrust or punch then go on the attack like the greatest fighter of all time. Or a lady who is overweight and in her dreams she is a top model in an incredible outfit that shows off her incredible slim body.

The best part of this is the fact that it all could become a reality if you truly put your mind to getting in shape mentally and physically. This is truly the time to be the person in your dreams, to become the person, fit and in shape, an incredible creator, athlete, or just an wonderful human being.

Many times our dreams can become true if only we were ready to get started by dedicating ourselves to the task that we have right in front of us. "I Had a Dream" was more than just a dream by Martin Luther King. It was a lifestyle which was set on making that dream come true.

One man, one dream, and the incredible results he was able to accomplish stand today. Just think about it. What do you really need to do in order to achieve your true and realistic goals? Imagine if you put your mind to do what it takes. You find yourself in a wave of internal exercise that allows you to respond in a positive manner.

Positive action. There is no substitute.

## Lonely and Confused

Positivity can help you when you are living in your head and wondering where you should go next. This happens to everyone. Using a positive approach to your life will help carry you through these times. The following is a look inside my brain and how I deal with myself.

Many days I'm by myself working on various projects, which is something I really enjoy. But there are days I really don't want to be alone. This urge to be among people is not bad because it never lasts long. Maybe five minutes. I think what I really need is to take charge over my prospective opportunities.

I should take time to really get single vision and focus, because the future looks incredible, with many opportunities for realistic success.

But that is my problem. There are too many things that I love to do, like producing a television series. Public speaking about things and people I love. Junior sports programs featuring youngsters from around the world. My radio show playing the music I love and interviewing people I enjoy communicating with.

Then there's after-school programs benefitting youngsters with homework assistance, exercise and nutrition. Making a movie about my sister, mother and grandmother. Revive my junior golf program. A movie about my BMX story. Retire (Oh hell no).

I would like to help my lady with her program. I have considered doing voice-over commercials. Read audio books. Act again on stage, television, motion pictures. I also envision creating an Olympic BMX Center with international events, after school programs and weekly competitions.

Those are just the important ones or most enjoyed. What makes it difficult is that I already did all of these successfully.
So if you were me, what would you really like to do?

I got it! But now is not the time to resort to confessions. I have had an incredible life. I've been to seventy-two countries in my life, have met and dated some of the most wonderful, and beautiful women of many different ethnic backgrounds. I've been married too many times, have five lovely children. I have grandchildren and great grand children, and will have great-great grandchildren before I die, and I'll be able to pick them up (if they let me) and understand them.

So what is the problem? I am living with the most wonderful lady in my life. For the first time, we understand, appreciate, enjoy, and love one another all at the same time. We sing (not always on key), dance, play golf (she got a hole in one - not fair), experiment on vegetarian dishes, exercise at least five days per week and laugh a great deal (not at each other).

We enjoy each other's company (we like to hold hands), communicate in a positive mode (more than ninety-eight percent of the time). We can have awesome conversations just about anywhere and anytime. So that part of my life is in place!

Ok, let's get back to what I should do. But the truth is I'm happy, very happy, but got to get going. I'm not getting younger, but I'm certainly not old. Thirty-two in the waist, 185 pounds, two-hour workouts almost daily, self-employed (no bosses, just partners) and loving life.

Working with young people is incredible, especially when they are achieving their goals, getting great grades, understanding life better, being good citizens at home and away from home, and headed for a positive future.

So why am I telling you all this? It's real simple. You see, I subscribe to the belief you can be great at everything you do if you put your heart and soul into it. Oh, and yes, you got to truly love it. You got to truly believe in it, you have to live it in your mind, roll up your sleeves, and live it in your heart and soul, and most of all, reality.

I really believe there is nothing in this world that you can't succeed at if you want it (really want it!), and you're willing to roll up your sleeves and make it happen.

So why do I not choose one and go for it? Real simple, I love it all. Everything listed. I love life. I love people (young and old). I have had success all my life in many different areas and never felt incompetent. I love people and I enjoy sharing air space with those that know a great deal and those wanting to learn a great deal.

Me? I'm a student of life because when you think you know it all, that's when you realize you really don't know as much as you think you do. I consider myself one of the luckiest people in the world.

So who am I? I don't know yet. I just know that I am in love with a wonderful lady, who's in love with me. I've accomplished a great deal but that's just parts of my life, and now it's time to really do something special.

Passing on the wonders life has provided you to others is important. Once there was a singing group that sang "Life Could Be a Dream (Sweetheart)." So true!

When everything shakes out, my confident, positive outlook on my wonderful life helps keep me invested and moving forward alongside those who are out there making things happen.

## Know Your Audience

To many people, identifying their "audience" becomes a natural response over time. We call this "maturing." Even though we may consider ourselves mature, intelligent people, we still need to be mindful of who we are speaking to and whether the conversation is to a single person or a multitude.

Did you know you can sow the seeds of success by simply maintaining positive words in your vocabulary and leaving out most of the negatives? This book delves into many life experiences where positivity has served me, whether I was in a good place or bad.

One of the most important things a presenter can do is to know and understand their audience in every way possible. There are obvious examples, of course, especially when they are broken down in the following manner:

1. Male
2. Female
3. American, Asian, African, etc.
4. Religion
5. Level of education (top and bottom)
6. Athletes
7. Atheist
8. Musicians
9. Racist
10. Pro-or against a specific group
11. Male and/or female executives
12. Clergy, plus denomination
13. Democrat/Republican/equally mixed or not

14. Feminist or not
15. Pro or against abortion
16. Anti guns, pro guns etc.
17. Stance on education

Regardless of who you are speaking to, you must respect their beliefs, their perspectives, and their experience.  If you are presenting to them, respect them.

If you choose to change them, respect where they are currently. If you want to enhance their beliefs, respect their views. If you want to merge groups of disagreeing mind sets, respect their individualism!

In presenting to any group, understand why they exist in their current fashion, their motto, ideology and public statements, identify them. Know them. If a particular group dresses differently from you, respect them.

You can show respect throughout any presentation, then at the end, comment with feelings of negativity toward them and lose their support. Respect them one hundred percent of the time. You are speaking to them. Don't think because you are not one of them, you don't have to respect them!

Respect is a strong component of positivity, wouldn't you say? When you take the time to know who you're speaking to, to direct words to them that will lift them up and help them, and on top of that, you show respect in every way possible, you will pave your own road to success.

## Know What You Need

Confidence. You do not achieve confidence through negativity. When you place positive thought, effort, and care into a project, good, and sometimes great, things happen.

Know what you need to be a success. Don't cut out important things. Don't compromise unless you really have to.

It was down to the wire time with the JAG BMX World Championship. The painters were painting the logos of our sponsors on the wooden jumps and starting hill. But this event was going to be indoors in Indianapolis.

It had begun to rain heavy and often. The painters informed me that I had to give them a name for the last big jump. I had been chasing Thom McAnn Shoes (at the time largest retail shoe store chain in the world). My contact was Mike Federman, CEO of the company.

Thom McAnn liked our program, but three things were not in our favor 1.) They never spent the dollars we requested on any event(s). 2.) It was the end of the year and their budgets were almost gone for the year. 3.) They had never seen this event (no one had. It was the first).

I was on the phone with my Thom McAnn contact discussing the importance of his commitment. The world would be introduced to Thom McAnn in one weekend. His response was very simple.

"Renny, I have only seventy-five dollars left in my budget for the year."

My mind was racing at that point. Questions in my mind were spinning at mach speed. We had Coca-Cola, 7-11, Bally Games, Hyatt Hotels, City of Indianapolis, a fast-food company, and hundreds of bike shops around the world.

I knew I wanted my own JAG BMX Shoe. Although Thom McAnn had said they were not interested in making a shoe for us, I knew they had never seen a major BMX race with parents, and kids not racing, but there to support their family members.

Family members! That was the key in all of this. Thom McAnn was the family shoe store! They needed to see this event.
So I told Mike Federman I would take the seventy-five dollars on five conditions. He reminded me that it was seventy-five point zero zero. Not hundreds. Not thousands. Just seventy-five dollars.

I told him I understood. So here are my "must haves" for accepting the seventy-five dollars.

1. I give your two sons a $1,300 JAG BMX Racing bike

2. I fly you and your two sons to Indie and the event

3. I put you and your sons into a suite at the Hyatt

4. I get you and your sons tickets to see the Harlem Globetrotters who will be in town

5. I will send a car to pick you and your sons up at airport and take you back to the airport.

Mike thought I was crazy, but said, "Yes." If you believe in what you are doing and know it is great, so will everyone else of importance, if only they can witness it least once.

The event was set with those on board and those I wanted to be on board. Thom McAnn had over 7,500 stores in the U.S. plus stores in Puerto Rico and other locations. This was an incredible opportunity and I was going to make sure it was going to work.

Mike called me three days later when the kids' bikes arrived. His kids couldn't wait to get to our event. They had begun to read up on JAG BMX, our event and our incredible team.

Mike and sons were picked up at the airport and registered into his suite. I was at the facility when he and his two sons with their passes around their necks walked in. At that very moment there were more than 4,000 BMX bikes turned upside down and being made ready for the event.

What a sight! The kids' jaws dropped and even Mike was amazed. It was going great so far, but there was much more to do. Mike and his kids watched the youngsters practice but soon he walked up to me with a very angry look on his face.

"Renny, there isn't one kid in here wearing Thom McAnn shoes or sneakers, and I'm supposed to be a major sponsor!"

Very calmly I reminded Mike he had become a sponsor only a few weeks before. I told him, "If you invite one of your stores to come down here and sell shoes and sneakers, we won't charge them for the space, nor ask for a percentage of sales."

I knew that the stores were very slow for the holidays. The first store showed up with a few hundred pair of shoes about two o'clock. By five o'clock he was sold out and jubilant and had his wife bring their kids down to the event. Step one accomplished. The dealers are going to be believers.

A second store came down. He sold out before practice ended. The next day, which was a Friday, four stores came down and took over a preset location for them, the Thom McAnn Shoe Center.

They sold out and stores from the outlying area were coming in. It was awesome! Mike left to go home with his kids beaming with positive and great remarks. Unknown to me, he told the CEO of the company everything that happened. But before he could tell the CEO, there were messages from the retailers that sold and the retailers that heard about it.

I must back up for a moment because I had been telling Mike ever since we met that it would be great to have a JOX JAG BMX Shoe. Mike was quick to let me know that Thom McAnn had never made a shoe with any other name on it than Thom McAnn, so don't get my hopes up for that to happen.
I still pressed every time we spoke. My phone at home rang early in the morning and it was Mike.

"How long will it take you to get to Worchester and meet with the CEO and President of the company?"

I had more than 25 kids staying at my home from around the world all due to leave in about three to four days. I told him within one week.

He said, "make it inside and get here. He's demanding a meeting asap!" and he hung up.

I called Mike back and asked if everything was alright? Mike told me he just got a major promotion, because sales are through the roof in Indie (Indianapolis). The CEO wants to become a national sponsor for JAG BMX.

As always I asked, "Can we make the JOX JAG BMX Shoe?"

Mike said, "No!" and hung up.

Meeting day came. As we were going up the elevator Mike said to me "Please don't ask about us making a shoe for you. It will only upset our Chairman."

Reluctantly I agreed. I met the chairman. I realized that this Hispanic man, Mike a Jew, and myself an African American, were the only minorities in the entire building. I chuckled without realizing it and the CEO said what's so funny?

I told him and Mike nearly crawled under the desk. The CEO had a big laugh and said "I was thinking the same thing!" After those remarks the meeting began. The first words from the CEO were "How would you like to have a Thom McAnn shoe with your name on it? A JOX JAG BMX Sneaker?"

I thought Mike was going to swallow the gum he was chewing. Question was how much for us? The CEO said how about ten percent of wholesale and my response was "how about 10% of ninety percent of the retail selling price." Both of them looked at me with surprise.

"Where did you get that number?" Requested the CEO.

My response was, "that's a common practice in the music business and is fair to everyone. We agreed and contracts were being made up. I was sent to the designers' office to discuss the look of our JOX JAG BMX shoe.

I drifted off for a few minutes reflecting on my decision to accept a seventy-five dollar sponsorship, give away more than $10,000 in rooms, air, free bikes, Globetrotter tickets, meals etc. Many would have called me crazy, but the truth is I believed in what we were doing.

I believed that if they witnessed the event, they would become a big sponsor. But I must be honest. I thought it would take up to a year for all this to happen. It took just a few weeks. Underestimated myself and team on that one!

When you take the time, energy, care, and positive belief in what you do to others, they will be impressed. They will catch your enthusiasm. When you deliver positivity, it attracts people. It does not matter if the person you attract is a CEO or a person starting out at the bottom rung. Positivity attracts good things and good people.

## If You Believe

Is it true that you can actually change your life by believing in yourself? You damn right you can.

Very exciting things occurred many times in my life. I think that most of these positives took place because I believed they could happen. Now that may sound crazy, but I have lived a dream life most of my life.

I had a great family, both parents with no divorces, separation, alcohol or abuse problems. In fact in many ways, outside of near poverty days in the very early years of my life, it was awesome. Throughout this book I've related to positive and wonderful instances that took place.

In comparison, there were not so great times even when financially things were great, family healthy, and all other necessities well taken care of. That might sound weird to many until you live this life and you begin to witness incredible wonderful highs with a few lows that are as deep as the highs were high.

But who is to say that variety is not the spice of life? Seriously, I remember days where hundreds of thousands of dollars in checks were in my drawers for weeks before getting to the bank or my accountant. I lived recklessly, although I never drank and did not do drugs. But I accepted every sweet moment life handed me.

There were times when simultaneously I was working on a multi-platinum recording artist's latest hit song, doing a television commercial, a television episode, promoting a concert with over 60,000 people, coaching my son's baseball game, my others son's soccer game and my daughter's singing, driving 120 miles round trip to my office, producing a motion picture, and exercising regularly, plus dating like crazy.

I remember doing a movie (Angela Davis story called "Brothers") in Bismark, North Dakota in December. The temperature dropped to fifty-seven below zero. There was a sign in our rental car that said if you run out of gas, burn your back seat for heat.

Coldest I've ever been in my life. There was only one woman on the crew and she was one of my best friends. No, I didn't sleep with her, but I sure made everyone jealous. I like people and they tend to like me for no other reason than I truly respect everyone until they give me a reason not to.

This was a perfect example in Bismark because I spoke to her like a real human being, not some uppity person because I was co-starring in a movie. She said the words that send most men chasing after a woman, "You are famous."

"No I'm Renny," I would answer, and she would laugh, and feel good about herself at the same time.

Treat everyone like they are special. Beginning with yourself, it really helps to know who you are, your good points, and bad. Addressing the bad ones should be one of your goals in life. All the while you should increase value to the rest of the world especially yourself.

Just think. I received preferential treatment at that hotel just for being nice to someone while others thought she came with the room package. Good thing I warned her in advance and that she was a quick learner.

I heard from her about three months after filming ended and she thanked me. She let me know she had gotten engaged to her high school sweetheart and was very happy. That was real good news and I was genuinely happy for her.

Unfortunately, I can't say I always took that attitude. There were enough times that I did which makes me feel good about who I am and how I have lived. How about you? Do you respect yourself and the people you come in contact with?

How about elders? Or those not as well off as you, those down on their luck, and those that have given up on themselves. It's amazing how a few choice positive words can ring out like huge bells all around you.

The positivity you share with others - that smile that sent a positive image to another across the room, in your arms, or holding your hand. How about just contemplating stepping off the deep end, into an awesome wonderful sea of love? How about understanding kindness and joy wrapped up into that person you have just claimed as yours for the rest of your life and having them affirm the same? Wow! It's magic no matter what age you are.

A quick story about a ninety-three-year-old man who works out every day in the pool. His wife passed away eight months prior to our meeting. It just so happened we met in front of my house and talked for a few minutes.

I invited him to come over to the house and he did. We spoke about sports, politics and exercise. Mostly he talked about his wife of many years.

I told him about what great physical shape he was in and the importance of his living out his years having a good time. We spoke for a few hours. I saw him just the other day coming from the pool. He told me hush-hush-like that he had a new girlfriend with the biggest smile, and happy soul.

No one knows how long he will be on this earth, but from the smile on his face he'll go to his grave smiling. Unbelievable!

What a wonderful world we live in. Enjoy who you are, and make yourself into who you want to be! Oh, and smile!

You damn right you can!

## If at First You Don't Succeed


Perseverance is a positive trait. Just because you don't get the right answer up front is no reason to quit a project you know will work. Too often we hit resistance and we walk away from something that could be huge.

It's true I took forty-two trips to Atlanta in order to get Coca-Cola to become my title sponsor, but the results were amazing. I became the Coca-Cola International Youth Sport Representative. I traveled around the world with members of our BMX Team and other endeavors.

I was the first to ever receive that designation from Coca-Cola. We promoted the Coca-Cola as the brand that really cares about young people and their families. Our message resonated with our diverse group of youngsters, from Hispanic, African American, Jewish, French, Japanese, and many other ethnic youngsters.

Yes, forty-two trips, each time driving home the virtues of my promotion featuring the gathering of youngsters, their families and their communities. A BMX champion is the envy of other youngsters around the world. He or she is definitely a hero in their own community.

In between each trip, we sought out ways to promote our project, which even included a sellout crowd (more than 18,000) at the Los Angeles Sports Arena. We made sure that the local Coca-Cola bottler was aware and supportive of our endeavors.

One bottler sent me a letter (I love this one), that announced they never thought we could pull crowds not once but five to six times in a row at the L.A. Sports Arena. It was hard for them to realize the magnitude of our accomplishments.

Yes we proved ourselves viable every time we hosted an event. I would create a promotion, invite all bottlers in the area, with free tickets for them and their family. When the event was over, I would ask them to share their feedback. I was always positive.

Before long the bottlers were convinced that we had the ability to draw crowds and bring loyalty to the Coca-Cola brand. I documented these results, then went back to Atlanta to present the results with support from the vocal bottlers.

The truth was, I was asking for a large sum of money. I needed the support and partnership of the bottlers through their willingness to support us. I needed the support of the home office with our national and international plans for the Coca-Cola JAG BMX World Championship.

By the time our series got off the ground internationally, we were being broadcast in over eighty-five countries, every military base, and ships at sea.

Bottlers all over the world were singing our praises and requesting our visit to their respective countries. But now, I'm getting ahead of myself, because that happened immediately after I signed with Coca-Cola.

The day of my forty-third trip to Coca-Cola was incredible. Almost as incredible as my forty-second visit. Mr. Dunn asked me to bring a proposal "about this thick" (he opened his fingers to about two inches).My reply was very simple (and I hoped it wasn't a deal breaker).

"Mr. Dunn, I don't have that much to say about my program. I've kept it very simple in order to maximize the results in the demographic markets we had promised to deliver."

Mr. Dunn looked at me and said, "That's ok. I have someone that will write it for you. Can you meet here in two weeks after the new presentation is ready?"

"Yes sir!" was my answer and two weeks later (seemed like a lifetime) I was in Atlanta at Coca-Cola USA in the main tower. I was wearing my best suit, shirt, and tie and came in the night before in order to get a good night's rest. Nothing, yes nothing, was going to stop me now.

I had a great product and had a demographic group worldwide. This group was active, involved the entire family, and never had a sponsor the size of Coca-Cola. They never had worldwide television and never had a world championship.

This was going to be awesome! I arrived one hour early and was ready! At least I thought I was. I thought this until I stepped into a conference room with thirteen of the most serious individuals I had ever seen in one room.

Everyone smiled politely and said their name. By the time the last man sitting said his name, I had forgotten all of them. Everyone seemed to have on black suits, white shirts and Coca-Cola ties. It was an incredible and scary sight.

Mr. Dunn introduced me and said, 'Go ahead Renny, tell us about your proposal.

I never opened the proposal. I never stopped talking. I told them about the sport, the events, and that almost every kid in America had a BMX bike. I told them about our annual Coca-Cola JAG BMX World Championship, and our Coca-Cola Series to take place strategically around the U.S. to attract all fifty states to our competitions.

I told them about our television series on ESPN. I told them about our team that was growing weekly with riders around the world. I told them that education played a role in the status of all our Coca-Cola JAG BMX "Official Team Riders" around the world.

I told them about our goal to televise our events in eighty-five countries, all military bases, and all military ships at sea. I told them that I would work twenty-four-seven to insure the success of our program and so would my crew and teams. I told them that we would be on television every Saturday of the week for fifty weeks per year.

I told them we would work with bottlers around the world who wanted bike safety, bike crazy, or bike racing in the parking lots of their largest customers. We were willing to offer a "Free Bike Give Away" in a drawing held on site with the bike delivered to the winner on the spot.

I told them that we would deliver television and live audiences worldwide with the same or similar program. It seemed like I had been speaking for an hour at least. It turned out to be forty-five solid minutes of what we would do for Coca-Cola. I was determined. I was fired up. I was not leaving with a "No!" Only a "Yes!" would do.

When I finished, Mr. Dunn asked me to please excuse myself from the room while they spoke to each other. As I was leaving the room, Mr. Dunn suggested I go to the bathroom. I responded I didn't need to go. In his inimitable way, he looked at me and said, "Yes you do."

I knew he was a powerful man, but knowing I needed to go was a bit much. I went anyway. I went straight to the sink and looked at myself in the mirror. I was loaded with sweat. My shirt looked like I had been hosed down.

I took off my jacket and tie. My entire shirt was soaked. I think it's called a sailor's bath. I got some paper towels, and rinsed myself. I dried with the hand blower. I also spent what seemed like an hour drying my shirt in front of the blower, and then put it back on.

I went back to the office and waited outside the room as instructed. I could feel the sweat coming back, even though the air conditioning was much more than adequate. Let's face it. The guys inside were wearing black suits, shirts, and ties. They never even glistened, much less got sweaty like me.

I was tired. "Bone tired" as my grandmother used to say. It seemed like hours had gone by. When I looked at my watch it had only been twenty minutes since I left the room.

Ten minutes later, Mr. Dunn walked out of the room and asked me to come in please. He asked in a formal manner that only Mr. Dunn could do. (On another note I always called him Mr. Dunn). I walked into the office and could not tell by their expressions if I had succeeded or failed.

All I knew was that I had given all I had at this meeting. I left it all on the floor. I looked up and smiled at everyone because I knew I gave my best-ever presentation.

One of the gentlemen stood up and said, "Congratulations, Mr. Roker and welcome to the world of Coca-Cola! We are proud to become your "Official Beverage Company." Mr. Dunn will give you all the information you will need and a contract."

At that point the sweating stopped. I could feel chills all over my body. Shortly after the meeting I contacted all the bottlers I worked with who contacted Mr. Dunn to say they wanted one of the televised events in their market. I thanked them for their support.

It was amazing! We would have our World Championship, ESPN television show and participants from around the world. We stepped up our promotion and put everyone on double duty. We contacted every country involved in BMX.

We worked out a deal with the Hyatt, our host hotel. Every country and state representative with twenty visitors or more would get a free room for themselves and their family. We had three months to go and all registration outside of the U.S. was signed up when you got there, fearing slow mail not arriving in time.

This was 1979, and mail from certain countries could take months. When we were leaving for Indianapolis, I asked Ernie "How many do you think we will get?"

"1,200 to 1,500," was his answer. 2,000 to 2,500 was my guess (but I always think big and that would have broken a record).

Two days before the event, Ernie said, "Renny, I miscalculated. I think we will have at least 3,000 participants and if we do we're in trouble.

"Why?" I asked.

"We are not capable of handling that many riders" he said. "That would be the all-time biggest BMX event ever!"

"Ernie, it is going over 4,000 riders. I haven't seen at least twenty of the countries that have confirmed to attend," I said. Can you imagine how big I was smiling?

If I had given up after the first, the third, the twenty-second or even the fortieth trip, the BMX World Championships may never have come into being. The sponsorship money and the television coverage for these events were unprecedented in this sport. Just goes to show you what positivity and perseverance can do…

## I Dream in Colors

Success is not dictated by race, religion, or any other external ridiculous prejudice. Success begins within. Learning how to tap into the success within yourself begins with a positive view of yourself and others. You cannot achieve this easily with preconceived discriminations.

As a young man, I have had the pleasure of knowing people from most countries in the world. What is unique is that they were all friends. At least they were friendly. Most of these individuals saw me as I saw them – friends.

What was unique about all of these people is the fact that we all got along quite well. As a matter of fact, many of us still communicate with each other over fifty years later. I find that I have more friends from different countries than I do in any state, or city in the U.S.

Another uniqueness is that the friends I've met around the world want me to return to their country and spend quality time together doing positive things and visiting with positive people.

Why is it different? Very simple. These are friends because they like me. Can they gain from these relationships? You bet they can! So can I. That's called a win-win situation.

What else is good about these relationships is the fact that no one feels they are giving or receiving in an unbalanced manner. The methods of performing in this manner is not taught, it is lived. Therefore, you have an incredible balance of friendship, respect, acceptance, and sharing.

When you get to that level it provides a quality of life that is unique, refreshing, rewarding, full of respect, and appreciative of your surroundings. It provides a sense of pride that permeates you with an incredible message to your audience. Most of all, it's a great message to yourself.

Success is when you are judged for your natural talent, your learned methods of operating by utilizing the people that support you, and recommend you, while you do the same for each of them.

When you reach out to assist, work alongside, and provide questions that generate questions and answers, unique relationships are built. This is a working relationship and camaraderie that you cannot dictate, demand or even suggest.

The power you generate, the respect you receive, the respect that you give, and the opportunity to use that power to rise with you, will bring success. You build a solid team that soon understands each others' strength and weaknesses and adapts accordingly.

This I have learned in my seventy-two years – that success bred through positivity is long-lasting, long-rewarding, and more easily attainable. I believe in people. I believe success lies within all our grasps if we would only reach for it – in a positive manner, of course!

## Helping Each Other, Can You Help a Brother?

I'm sure it's easy to conceive the fact that helping each other is a positive trait. What happens though, when money, or prestige, or power come into play? From my perspective, this is where positivity can boost everyone. A lack of positivity will tear it apart.

Almost every ethnic group has a tendency to look out for each other, respect each other, and support each other's positive activity. But that's not necessarily the truth all the time.

I had an incredible relationship with a major corporation and was receiving large sums of money on a regular basis for a promotion that was profitable for this company. It increased the popularity and respect for the company.

One day I was speaking with a couple of friends when a great idea was shared for my corporate sponsor. After listening intently, I realized this was an excellent idea. I offered to introduce my friend to some high level executives at my sponsor's office. Everyone agreed.

After my friend with the project left, my other friend looked at me and asked me if I was crazy. He said that our friend, whom I offered to help, could be getting dollars that I could have for my projects.

I looked at him and asked him if he was crazy. If I send my sponsor a great package like he has, guess what? They are going to thank me for recognizing a need and fulfilling it for them. Also, they will recognize me for not being so greedy that I won't share an opportunity for them from a friend.

I looked at my friend and in the most sobering voice I told him, "You need to wake up. When these companies realize that you are interested in their well-being and bottom line, you are important to them. But if by the same token you feel it's best to not include your corporate supporter and benefactor because of greed, you're not ready to support your own people. It becomes apparent that you don't have any loyalty to anyone but yourself.

There are too many people who feel like you do, and that's one of the reasons why we have such a difficult time trying to do business with anyone, including each other. It's time to be proud and share! Know that when everyone benefits, they all win, especially the person who gets it started – you!"

Total focus on personal gain is not related well to positivity. Yes, you can see some short-term success here, but shortcuts rarely keep you in the game for the long haul. Be willing to step up and do the right thing by your brother, your friend, your colleague, your co-worker. Positivity breeds long-time success for all.

**Getting a Royal Spanking**

For those of you in my age bracket (over 70), I'm sure you have come under the thunder of a mother or father that spanked you at least a few times. The funny thing about spanking, I never saw it as or felt like it was abusive.

As a matter of fact, those times when I was able to escape spanking, I usually had my own form of celebration internally. But the spanking that broke the record for my sore behind was the time I was asked to wash the dishes. Instead, I put them in the garbage and went off to play in a very important ball game.

My mother arrived at the ball park and watched the entire game. She cheered the loudest for me. When I hit a double you could hear her in the entire park, "That's my son!" I heard her tell anyone that would listen.

I actually thought that the better I played and the more she got excited about my outstanding playing (at least I thought it was worthy of praise), the less likely I would get punished or spanked. I got lucky and hit an "in-the-park-homerun."

My mother went crazy hooping and cheering. "That's my son!" She couldn't be prouder and I couldn't be either. Amazing what fear of an ass whipping from the end of a switch can do to you. It was just not my idea of fun.

So on my last at bat, I hit the longest ball I ever hit in my life and began showing off as I rounded the bases. I heard my mother sing out, "Boy, don't you dare act like that to the other team. Be a gentleman."

The crowd went wild cheering for my mom. Being the shy
woman she was, she quietly sat down and smiled broadly with
motherly pride. By this time I thought my mom had forgotten
all about the dishes in the garbage and a few other items I
neglected to do because I got up late.
She did not forget. She told me as we were walking home,
excited about the game I just played. My mom told me that she
was very proud of me except my taunting of the other team.

My smile widened as I just knew that I had done enough great
things to eliminate any spanking. Boy was I surprised, because
out of nowhere the strap appeared. I got one healthy swat on
my bottom. I also got a smile from my mom as she told me
how proud she was of my accomplishments.

She spent a great deal of time reminding me that we could one
day be in the same position as the other team next time we play
each other. Could I accept my behavior coming from the other
side as we lost the game?

"No way would I accept that. I would play my heart out to
win," I said.

My mom looked me straight in the eyes and spoke, "And what
makes you think the other team would not fight back next time
you played? What makes you think you have not made them
angry enough to never forget what you did to them?"

I put myself in their position for the first time. I realized what I
had done. I asked my mom what she thought I should do?

"Apologize," was her response. "And do it now and right
before that next game. Let them know you respect their ability
and the team. Get them to like you and respect you. Go out and
beat them with a friendly smile, not a rude attitude."

It took me a while to understand my mom's message. As I got
older her explanation had greater meaning and understanding.
At one point I thought, *how did my mom know so much about*

*playing teams in baseball?* Later I realized that this wasn't a baseball situation, this was one of life's situations. Wow! My mom was awesome! And this wasn't the only thing she and or my dad taught me in their own inimitable way of expressing life's incredible highs and lows. They taught me about reality and falsehoods, life and living/existing in this world, and how to face the many challenges.

Positivity comes into play even in "discipline" moments, whether these moments are delivered by a parent or yourself. Learning how to interact and treat others in a positive way sometimes calls for painful lessons. These lessons keep coming our entire life, so be open and ready to learn at all times.

**Choosing the Path of My Future**

I've always worked hard and long in everything I did and never thought about it much until one day my son asked me, "Why do you work so hard dad?" It made me stop and think about the true answer.

Working hard was always the way I worked, striving for excellence, and enjoying the thrill of success. I loved my work, whether it was on the radio, public speaking, promoting concerts, promoting and selling records, acting or producing sports events.

These were all aspects of my personal life that I thoroughly enjoyed. What was so fantastic was the fact that they were all exciting jobs. Each required total concentration and attention. I looked at my son, whom I loved so much.

It's amazing how you can get engrossed in your work and lose sight of those you care about, especially when you are a single parent. Whoever said that raising a child, running a household and a business, trying to have a social life, was easy?

This is unbelievable. I have so much respect for women! Yes I said it! I have so much respect for women. They're able to run a household, fix meals, do laundry, treat little cuts and bruises, review homework, and assist in finding answers to questions. I respect women!

Just think about the myriad things that women do while men sit on the couch watching television. Especially when she works eight hours a day outside the home also.

I learned how to iron clothes early in life (high school). I learned how to wash dishes, clean, and even fix the simple problems in a home (no I'm not a real fix-it man!). I'm a good guy for a great woman (yes I have one now). Why do I say that?

Very simple. I iron the clothes that she washes (What a team). I polish the floors (wood), and fill the dishwasher. I even cook, plant flowers, and attempt to clean and arrange my office (boy do I have lots of stuff in my office).

Size is not important in the world of success, only the size of your heart and will to succeed. Here's a story of a man that went against common opinion and succeeded tremendously. He was a man who maintained a great attitude towards others

Many people know Casey as the creator, moderator, and announcer of American Top Forty. Many used to wait anxiously for Casey to come on the air to see who had the top music. The originator of this incredible program that seemed to last a lifetime was Casey Kasem. He may have been small in stature, but he was a giant as a friend.

I remember when Casey first started on radio in Los Angeles. It was station KFWB. He was on late at night. This was a man who everyone loved and teased and considered brilliant. He created  American Top Forty. He was heard all over the U.S. and around the world. Casey wrote the book on syndicated radio. He was one of the most popular disc jockeys on radio.

All the popular jocks at this early stage of radio laughed at hosting this kind of program, much less syndicate it. Casey knew just what he was doing. I used to visit him from time to time at the station. Put simply, Casey was my link to big time radio in sunny California.

Unfortunately, he recently died. Wow! What a good and great man.

I remember one of Casey's favorite lines. In most cases, it came as a phone call from him to me with Casey saying, "Renny. Hurry up or you'll miss the opportunity."

This all started one day when Casey called me out of the blue and said, "Renny. Don't you do voice-overs?"

I said, "Yes."

Casey gave me an address and the directions to, "Get my ass over there right now!" It was an interview for Gallo Wine and I got the spokesperson job. He warned me against joining all their parties because I didn't drink then and still don't.

Whenever I asked for advice, his response was, "Do the best you can and put a smile in your voice." Well I got the job and it lasted about five years as the voice of Gallo Wine (that was hot!)

Shortly after I got the Gallo job, I received another call from Casey. This one took me right over the top. Apparently Casey had been doing voices for the "Super Friends" television program. They needed a new voice for several episodes. He asked if I were interested.

As soon as I said, "Yes!" he gave me the address. He told me to hurry or someone else would get the parts.

What a great day working side by side with Casey for over three years. Those were great times. We had lots of great conversations.

Casey Kasem cared about people. That was very obvious, in his mannerisms and conversations. Most of all, in a face-to-face meeting, you knew he was a great man, small in size but huge in heart!

So as you plot your path in life, remember Casey and relate his memory to positivity. Casey took on something huge, far bigger than himself, and he defined his path well. Remember, opportunity is fleeting. Like Casey said, move quickly. I like to think I've defined my path and legacy well – with a willingness to act with a strong dose of positivity!

## Create Loyalty to Keep Sponsors/Partners

Of all the things that I have done in my years of creating, producing, televising, broadcasting sponsors, supporters, investors etc., the moment you make any and all of these people feel you really love their brand, their product, their image and your relationship, you've achieved something of significant value to everyone. That's positivity.

Let's begin with sponsors because I really love sponsors. They put up hard cash, and goods. Where would Coca-Cola be if all the theaters had Pepsi product? If you owned a theater and chose a certain brand for that theater, it's generally because of personal taste, a good price, or who you think will satisfy your customers!

In other words, it's all about who has done the best job to positively influence a potential customer. Beginning a long term relationship with sponsors, clients and supporters is a very involved, but not complicated world to exist in.

To be begin with, ask yourself a simple question, "If it were me, what would I want a person to do or say and why? Then take that thought and put it up alongside the person or company you want to impress. Keep it simple. Keep it honest. Keep it easy to digest in every way.

Don't attempt to attract a company because you don't like their competitor. In this day and age, the person you sell at company "A" could be working for company "B" tomorrow. The key is respect for the individual, respect for the company, respect for their ideology and direction.

Make sure you are able to demonstrate that you have what they need to make their company more profitable or better brand recognition. Realistic steps lead towards success.

It's very important that you can clearly express defined steps that increase their positive exposure. In most cases, businesses understand that unless they are hosting one of those incredible sales promotions, "Open at Midnight" and "Most Product Valued at $1,000 is now $10" kind of promotion is not what you are offering.

What works is a gradual increase in business and loyal customers, based on a quantified program that makes sense to the client. Most companies have heard and seen the "one day wonders" that claim to change companies overnight. Sell realistic and work your hardest to make it bigger.

If you achieve your goal, you are a man or woman of your word. If you out-do your predictions, you are definitely a "keeper" in the eyes of the person and the company. You are building a bond and respect level that will be passed on to others in your industry.

You are not a "one day wonder" but a for-sure "lifetime producer." This is, to me, the secret to success and a positive relationship with sponsors. They, in many ways, become your partners as you enhance each other's position and bottom line.

This brings to mind another aspect of this. The person you are selling must give you room to breathe in your dealings. If you can't make money because the deal is too one-sided, it doesn't work. If it doesn't work, you should not do it because eventually you lose later.

Win now and stay a winner. Have a real conversation with your client, sponsor, or supporter. Spell out the facts and what is really expected. Then work your hardest and smartest to outdo your prognostication. Now that's where the euphoria comes in, satisfying your sponsors, your partners and most of all your own self worth.

Results are very simple to explain. The majority of partners, friends in industry, sponsors, will return and most of the time bring another partner or company to join them. Make them believe! Make them feel good about your results, not your talk! Deliver. Deliver. Deliver. Then reap the benefits of your hard work, clear thinking, and "Sticktoittivity!" (in English never quit).

In order to make long-term sponsorships and partnerships work, positivity MUST be in your life, your decisions, and your relationships, both personal and professional. With positivity permeating your life, you will find those you need to move forward.

## Doing What is "Right"

I've mentioned a program I ran called "Teens on the Green."
We had members around the world. We had events in
Colombia, Thailand, Virgin Islands, Europe, Canada, Russia,
six African nations, Australia, Somoa, Brazil, Myanamar and
many more.

We had students that received scholarships based on grades to
Stanford, Penn State, UCLA, USC, and over 100 other
universities and colleges. Our motto was, "Where high grades
and low scores really count." We meant that. In order to be on
the team you had to have a "C" average or better. In addition,
students had to have a twelve handicap or lower. That was just
the beginning.

Our members were from every ethnic background in the world,
male and females. Getting in was easy and we traveled often.
For a long time we had an airline sponsor. When we first
started, Miami's World Famous Doral Hotel was our home
course. World Famous Instructor Jim Mclean was our honorary
coach. Many of his coaches worked with our team members.

Everyone had to bring their clubs to practice and play. Those
were the clubs that got them a twelve handicap and lower.
Their report cards or official grades letter from their respective
schools was required.

In the beginning, many students asked, "Where are my clubs?"
as if we were going to give them new clubs. They could earn
them. That required increased Grade Point Averages and
decreasing their handicap from what they had, especially since

they were getting lessons from some of the best golf instructors in the world.

The students were training on one of the world's greatest golf courses and receiving tutoring to increase grade point averages. Everyone had to assist their team members. They were not competing against each other they were competing with themselves and the goal was to get better!

One day I was sitting watching about thirteen youngsters chipping at the same spot for hours. A few came over to me and said why won't they let me hit with my driver?

*Good question* I thought, so I asked the coach privately. His answer was unique. He said that he wanted to see them "Hit the ball."

I said, "They're hitting lots of balls."

"But not the right ball," he responded, then continued, "I have thrown out a ball about 25 yards away and I want them to hit that ball, preferably on the run rather than through the air."

I got it. If you can hit the ball from that or closer distance, you can save at least one stroke and usually more. Doing that eighteen times per round is extraordinary. I walked over to the grumbling group and said, "I recommend all of you find a way to hit the ball he threw out not once but at least three or more times.

It could mean saving many strokes that will get you into the playoffs, or finals and possibly an outright win. This part of the lesson definitely increases your ability to focus, so I suggest you pay close attention to this incredible practice that can help you immensely."

Seems like just moments later I heard a few then more and more whoops and exaltations of success. I watched the "hit the ball group" grow stronger. One young man came to me and said that was the best practice he ever had. I looked at him and asked him one question, "Can you repeat that in the middle, beginning, end or throughout a competition?"

I loved his answer. "Not without more practice like this regularly."
In one particular group of youngsters, there was a very interesting young man. He went to a huge contest at Disney Golf Courses in Orlando every year for the past four years. Each year he would finish last in that year's age group.

I knew this story, but did not want to discuss it until he was ready and could ask or answer the question as to "Why me?". For some reason, when he told me he was going to this event for the fifth time, there was a look on his face that did not look like another disaster weekend, but just the opposite.

I told him to enjoy himself and have fun. He looked at me and said, "Winning is fun."

I agreed. I also reminded him that enjoying yourself is fun, especially when you know what you're capable of accomplishing. All weekend I wondered how this young man would do this year. I didn't have to wonder long because I saw his parents getting out of their car with him on the way to my front door.

Both his mom and dad asked forgiveness for coming to my house unannounced, but David wanted to tell me something. He stepped forward and pulled from behind his back a Second Place trophy and the biggest smile I've ever seen. I could feel the tears of joy welling up inside me.

He was so happy and proud. He was a new young man that now believed in himself. And yes, he earned a scholarship to college a few years later.

Never give up on a dream just because it doesn't come true the first time you wake up. Positivity is a concept and reality that is fun and enjoyable, just like the young man's golf experience. Positivity calls for practice. Patience. Concentration. Choice. Choose the wisest path available to you. Positivity is a daily decision you must make.

## Conflict Resolution

Have you ever wondered why it is so important to you that everyone in the room "like you", thought you were a really nice person, or told you, "I'm glad you are here." and meant it?  Have you been disappointed because you were not asked to go to lunch or to meet later?
Why was this so important?  Why did you feel that funny knot in your stomach as you waited for the damn invitation to take place?  Who the hell did you think you were anyway?

You do not belong to their group. You do not dine or hang out with them. You don't even talk to them on the phone from time to time. What if they did call you to speak? What would you talk about?

Would you answer the questions honestly?  Would you tell them what you felt rather than what you thought they might want to hear?  Do you really give a damn, or are you just playing stupid mind games?

There were lots of things going through my mind. I had to make a decision.  Do I say what I think they want to hear or do I speak from my heart and soul?  It was important to me that they realized that I wanted to make a difference for this organization.

I liked what they were trying to accomplish.  I knew they wanted to succeed, and I had a feeling that they were trying so hard to imitate another organization.

I told the truth, I told them how I felt about the direction they were taking. I told them that I realized they wanted to be better than the other group, but the only way they could get better would be by enhancing what they do best, and maximizing the productivity of each member of their organization. Join forces with the other group if desired but don't try to destroy each other.

There was silence in the room as one young man stood up and said, "I have been thinking about our direction for quite some time, and realized that we had gone astray from our original plans.  I realized that we were competing with a group with similar, yet different goals. I realized that we were weakening our core by following others who are similar, but not the same."

For a while there was silence in the room as many squirmed in their seats.  You could see these great minds thinking about this conversation.

One by one they each stood up and talked about their original goals, which began to change as their popularity grew closer to what they deemed "The Competition", "The Enemy" etc.

With both operating in concert with each other, the only result could be a dynasty of two separate companies that provided a unique service to their customers.

At that moment the energy changed in the room and the conversation became higher and higher with an incredible burst of continuous energy that permeated even the walls of this large room with all of their positive energy.

All of a sudden there was a light of positivity in the room. Ideas were going from one to another, and each other as if a bolt of high powered energy had hit each of the participants. For hours they went over carefully, the new plan, the revised new plan, the creative new plan, the incredible new plan, the realistic and doable new plan. The plan that would spell success. Finally they realized that they had become their own competition and was having problems getting out of their own way.

The celebration was incredible as the direction was set down with everyone's approval. A call was made to the "used to be competitor" to discuss working in concert with each other.

Both companies rocketed rapidly upwards through the ranks enjoying themselves and their new associates. Eventually they joined forces and their values increased significantly.

It doesn't matter if it's two major corporations or two individuals.  Sometimes we deem the other person as the "Competition", "The Enemy", "Oh, Those Guys" etc. when sometimes they could just as easily become an ally.

Funny, the other day I asked my plumber if he knew a good electrician?  He pulled a card out of his wallet and handed it to me.  He told me that they each represent close to 50% of each other's business by referring each other.

Isn't that something? Two people helping each other.  If you listen clearly to those you meet every day, you will find from time to time there is an opportunity to be an asset to each other. This usually only happens with a positive attitude!

## Positivity

It's been years since I was in elementary school in New York, high school in the Virgin Islands and college in Puerto Rico. I bussed tables in New York then proceeded to work for Nat "King" Cole promoting his last hit record "Rambling Rose". Positivity is about not giving up on things you believe in. Positivity in your life, your work, your play and creative moments is essential in order to grow and succeed. Easier to say than to do some would say, but guess what? There are too many people who have been successful from every race, creed, and economic situation to make it easy to believe that everyone is capable of succeeding. But only if they believe in themselves.

There are those that begin a project on Monday, and if it is not worth millions by Friday, they give up and start another project. Not too smart. And not conducive to any kind of success.

"Positivity" is an extreme, powerful confirmation of working for success, regardless of elements that try to stop it or change it.

Positivity is the most beautiful "state of mind" you can ever encounter. No matter what the situation is "positivity" can make it work. "Positivity" can put you in a state of mind that will help you believe in yourself.

1. You are as great as you think you are (providing you have "fine tuned" what you consider your assets).

2. Keep looking for ways to better yourself and communicate with those who are seeking the same positive results.

3. Find the best way to join forces with others that are positive in mind and production.

4. Stay positive even when things seem to be going in the wrong direction.

I remember shortly after a horrid divorce and the loss of two of my three children to their mother, I was sitting down with my son discussing, "What we are going to do next?" We spoke about taking a long drive. We went over his "wish list." We talked about making changes to the house or moving to the Caribbean where I once lived. We talked about many other possible actions and traveling.

I was broke and whipped. I looked at my son and began to explain a meeting coming up later that day that could realize $40,000 for me (us!), and a possible movie that would pay around $500,000. There was also some promotion work, plus a sporting event that I was working on. It was so easy to say this.

Kelly looked at me and shook his head, "Dad. How can all that happen in one day?"

I told him even more than that could happen in one day if you let it! I got dressed and took off for Hollywood and my meeting. I returned with a check for $40,000. I got an offer on my ranch. I also landed a potential movie contract.

*Not a bad day,* I thought. My son didn't believe any of it till I showed him the check for $40,000 and the script for the movie.

My son and I went out for dinner. He was always so positive. He believed in me. I enjoyed communicating with him.  We still talk like friends, with a very unique understanding that we are father and son.

Positivity. Great things are born of this concept. Work. Family. Relationships. Education. Life.

The more you grow with respect and pride for yourself, family, friends and co-workers, and even competitors, the greater the opportunity for success.

What is success? In my life, I've seen the truth that success is best bred through positive motivations. Success is not wealth. Success would better be defined by the positive footprint we leave on this earth.

Success is self enjoyment, respect, family harmony, money, friends and great referrals when seeking new or additional employment, deals, or partners. Success is pride in your every way, everyday!

Only you can reach success for you with the assistance of those that respect, admire, and love you! Keep positivity in your life and use it as your key to unlock YOUR door to success!

# About the Author

Renny Roker was born in
the Bronx, New York, but lived a
significant portion of his younger
days in the Virgin Islands and
Puerto Rico. He has one brother
and two sisters. Renny loves to
talk. At the age of 14 he was a full
time Disc Jockey on the radio in
the Virgin Islands where his
family moved to when he was 12
years old. He still likes to talk.

Renny has settled down "for the rest of my life" with Linda in
Flagler Beach Florida where he runs, rides his bicycle and
plays golf in between scores of meetings and promotions.

He still has the fire to keep forging forward. Renny is very
interested in helping young people step up and into their
potential. Most of all, Renny maintains his POSITIVE
ATTITUDE! One of his most important goals is to make life
better for youngsters of all ethnic backgrounds. He also desires
to work with adults that need encouragement to make their
lives better for themselves and their children.

Renny plans to create an "After School" homework and
recreation center for youngsters and motivational talks with
adults to enhance their belief in themselves while satisfying
their employers with better attitudes and positive production.

CPSIA information can be obtained at www.ICGtesting.com
Printed in the USA
LVOW06s2331070815

449080LV00007B/64/P